CHERISH HER

"My Mother and I" Series

ALNITA JOHNSON   ELLA MAE MONTAGUE

DOROTHY MONTAGUE FOSTER   CARLENE HILL BYRON

DR. DIANE SUBER   DEANGELA PERRY   PEGGY TATUM

SHINA MILLER   NINA OTERIA   SOPHIA DOWNING

MARILYN ROGERS   MARILYN BRYANT-TUCKER

JOANN ROBERTS   ANTONIO MCCARVER   ALEXIS J. GREEN

APRIL DOZIER   TAJALA LOCKHART   DEBRA ROBERTSON

GLORIA V. DEBNAM   MICHELLE GREEN-KING

KAREN JONES   ARLINDA RODRIGUEZ

BETH WRIGHT-JEFFERSON   MARSHA PERRY

VALISHA SUMMERFIELD   NESE HOPSON

PASTOR LOWRAY BARTNEY   AGNES SANDERS PENNY

STACIE PATTERSON   NIKKI TURNER   MONIQUE THOMAS

PARRIS SOLOMON

Cherish Her (Anthology) ©2017 by Alnita Johnson

ISBN: 978-1546621201

Manufactured and Printed in the United States of America

ACKNOWLEDGMENTS

Thanks Mom

I dedicate this to my mom, Ella Montague. I wrote her story inside.

She gave her life, her dreams for her children.

We are a talented bunch; all of us: Tonya, Shae, Al Jr. (aka Joe-Joe) and me. We sing, draw, paint, build, teach, etc. We are entrepreneurs, business owners, hair stylists and barbers, makeup artists and more.

My mom though would stand back and ask, "What is my gift?" My Mother's gifts weren't very strong in any of the demonstrative areas; she wasn't a visual artist like my dad or musically inclined like her children. I would always say to her that she was the BEST mom ever! She would smile and sometimes, a tear would fall, as if she didn't believe it was enough.

I told her about the seven Mountains of Influence; the seven areas that influence culture, which are Religion, Education, Government, Media, Arts & Entertainment, and Business. Because, when I understood that every person was called to one or more of these mountains, I immediately knew that my mom was called to the Family Mountain. The "Family Mountain" is the "building block" of community and strong theme throughout the Bible. God has always desired that families unite together as one in Him. When my mother understood that she too had purpose, and when she found her place in Him, joy and fulfillment began to flow. You see she was and still is operating successfully in her purpose, which is to first, teach every one of her children about Jesus planting the seed for God to work in and grow. She has always been virtuous and dutiful as a wife and mother; a true example of a MOTHER. My family and generations to come will continue to be blessed because of my mother's love.

INTRODUCTION

The Bible says that the older women should teach the younger and yet, I am not so sure that is happening.

The images that flash across the television and social media can portray women in some of the most unflattering ways. Yet God says that we are "fearfully and wonderfully made" (Psalms 139:14) and that is without a doubt. It is my belief that to crawl around in the low places and eat what is for the serpent is not our God given portion. We are the mothers of nations and kings and the nurturers of civilization. I believe placed inside every woman's DNA, inside her XX chromosomes God placed everything needed to influence and change our lives and ultimately the lives of a generation.

Throughout history, God has used women to bring hope and inspiration to many a valiant man in our society past, present and future. We are influential and have an innate ability to turn the hearts of the kings.

Is the older woman's wisdom outdated? Modern parenting philosophies and "new age" ideologies have run amuck and have been proven detrimental. They create adult children who are narcissistic and without a clear sense of reality. Because of this, families are starting to return and revisit some of the tried and true methods of our parents and grandparents. Many of these "tried and true methods" are just that—tried and true. They really work! This is what inspired me to write this book.

Last year several of my close, personal friends and clients lost their mothers and I began to wonder how the lack of "mama's" wisdom could be devastating; not just for me, but for others like me and for generations to come. When I thought about the multitude of wisdom overflowing in the cemeteries that could have helped some young mother avoid a terrible tragedy, I knew I had to do something.

So, I asked daughters, sisters, sons and husbands to write short stories about their mothers, grandmothers, aunties and the mothers of their children. I posed the question, "What did you learn from your mother? They were free to tell the good, the bad and the ugly. I asked it this way because in any situation we can learn how to be as good as our mothers or rather to avoid some of her mistakes. Parenting does not come with a manual—it is simply learned through trial and error—and can always be improved upon. Isn't this what life's all about; learning and improving? These stories will make you laugh and cry as the writers recount special moments in their personal history. It is my sincere hope that as you read each person's story, you will allow yourself to walk, for just a few moments, into the lives of the author. I hope that you will read something that will illuminate the lives of your children, your mother, yourself while also gaining some wisdom that may enhance your life.

THE MATRIARCH

Matriarch (noun)

1. *The female head of a family or tribal line.*
2. *A woman who is the founder or dominant member of a community or group.*
3. *A venerable old woman.*

Let us all celebrate the matriarch. Mom, Mother or Ma, whatever you may call her, is so much more than "just" mom. Some may describe her as A ruler, dignified woman, Grande dame, matron, queen... ancestor. How much dignity and honor these words bring to mind. However, in this modern society, the term "Mother" is not be used in the same endearing way. "Back in the day" there was definitely going to be a brawl if someone dared talk about a son's mother. But today...

In large numbers of families, mothers are the dominant figure even when dad is around. She is the one who pulls things together; the glue the makes the family stick. Even dad relegates many of his decisions to mom because he knows she has a better handle on the pulse of the family. When we were children, we would role play her decision-making processes in games such as "Mother May I." However, unlike the game, the real life consequences for not obeying mom were intense. She demands respect because she knows that she has given her all for her family. Her love is strong and endures many hardships and heartaches, but a real mom never gives up on her seed.

God creates every person for a purpose far greater than what we imagine. This also includes women. We cannot ignore the light shining ever so brightly within.

We must live our lives with our eyes wide open, having complete knowledge that God is doing something gigantic and He has decided to use us.... WOMEN!

We are not hiding any longer!

Run and tell the story for the entire world to hear. Lift out voices and shout aloud! We now understand that we can "bring home the bacon, and fry it up in a pan and still never let you forget you're a man," because we are women, and it's okay! You can hear the roar of our collective voices piercing the darkness with a fierceness that only God can give.

We will not be silent anymore!

We are well able, capable partners working together with you husband, man, brother, lover and we are aware that you know this. We understand that without us, you would be incomplete and not only without your socks... smile (wink).

Our heightened spiritual ears are sensitive to the Father's calling and quick to respond. Just like the young sapling in the Father's hand, we easily bow and bend. For this reason He has made us to be the joyful mother of children.

We not only have biological offspring, but our God-given purpose and vision incubates and delivers many spiritual sons and daughters. We no longer walk in shame but stand boldly in the Blessing, ever increasing in everything and everywhere we go. WE have, as it were, "the golden touch."

Young Mother, do not cover your head in shame. God is our

redeemer, husband, and lover (Isa 54:5). For this we, women, wife, mother are thankful. We are eternally grateful. We are yours, Lord. We are always yours.

Read each story with an open heart looking for the treasures found inside. When you find an area that touches your heart, apply ointment of wisdom there and watch healing take place.

My prayer: Father allow those who read this book be touched with your love. May shame, guilt, bitterness, and unforgiveness fall away, as the reader turns every page; and may your love and GRACE wash over them. Help the reader have a deeper understanding for Mom. May all the broken places be healed in Jesus name! -Amen

Much Love,
Alnita Johnson

SHE LOVES... FLAWS AND ALL

Alnita Johnson

I remember reading in my Baby Book where my mother writes, "Alnita always grabs the candy dish." She would tap my hand and say, "No, No." "She always knew I'd come back to it", she wrote. I smile, thinking about the young woman my mother once was.

It was 1970 and times were quite different than they were now. My mom and dad were both from small towns in North Carolina. She from Varina, (now Fuquay-Varina) and him from Knightdale. My mom, the only girl in a family of seven boys, found out she was pregnant. My dad, already having experienced pain and disappointment in his own father, didn't want his firstborn child, nor the mother of his child to journey down a road he found all too familiar. Bravely, he asked my grandfather James, my mother's father, if he could have my mother's hand in marriage, and consequently, all six my mother's brothers. They consented, as He was a good choice and well liked. So, In early spring, my mother and father, both of modest means were married at the reverend's home surrounded by a host of family and friends.

Flipping through the pages of my parent's wedding and honeymoon album, I can see the glow in my mother's eyes. She is dressed in a beautiful baby blue mini wedding dress, matching sheer hose and sling-back pumps; her veil covers her face, but her big brown eyes shine with excitement and bliss. On this day, she was happy. I was told that my dad was so nervous when placing the rings on her finger that he shook. Which was material for the reverend's comic relief during the wedding.

"With this ring, I thee wed..."

She looks into my dad's eyes with all the hopes and dreams any young woman has of better. Better than what her mother experienced. My mom was always optimistic that things would get better and maybe because of this outlook, they did.

My mom often speaks candidly to us, her children, about her experiences growing up in Varina. She talked about having to share beds with her brothers and yet, they were able to have the utmost respect for each other. She talked about having to stand up for her baby brother Nathaniel sometimes, even though she was a girl. She was never scared. Maybe it was because she knew that somewhere not too far behind was her five bigger and stronger brothers, who would come to her rescue if she needed. They loved "Doodla", my mom's nickname.

My mom would often talk about the abuse my grandmother suffered in the home and yet, like most of the women of that time, she stayed. She talked about the liquor house they operated and how talented a carpenter my grandfather was. He had designed a chair that had a hidden compartment inside. When there was a search on the home, my grandfather would sit my mother atop the chair and whisper to her not to move. She did as instructed because she trusted her father. How complex a love that must have been? My mom loved her parents dearly. Her mother worked tirelessly to provide whatever she and her brothers needed. While my grandfather for reasons not full known, worked full-time but would keep most of his income for himself. For example, on Saturday's when my grandmother had to work at the local restaurant, my mom and her brothers would have to wait until she returned home to eat, while her dad would eat hoop cheese in front of them.

My mother has the uncanny ability to always see the best in people and not disapprove too much. She noticed enough to recall the hunger pains but forgiving enough to give her father space to change. That is amazing love!

When her mother comes home from work my mom runs and tells her mother about how hungry she has been all day. I don't know how many times this happened, but the image of my grand-daddy cutting that hoop cheese and eating it while her stomach was growling made a lasting impression on her young mind. She did not like that one bit! She did not hesitate letting her mom know about her displeasure immediately when she comes home. As the only girl, she felt that she had to make her voice heard. Her parents didn't discourage that either. I guess that's where I get that outspokenness. And even though her father would be insensitive to their needs at times, you would hear her speak more about the times that he would openly demonstrate how fiercely he loved. I guess in her eyes one greatly outweighed the other. Eventually she would come to realize that both her mother and her father were flawed people doing the best with the tools they were given. She loves her parents for who they are flaws and all.

This kind of love fueled my mom's love for her children. I will always remember how my mom enjoyed playing sports with us. On every level, she was an involved parent. If we had to rake leaves, clean the house, do yard work, she was right there with us. She did not believe in telling us what to do and not participating in it herself. She would often tell us that growing up as the only girl; she would get so upset because her brothers were always on the go and seemed to do less while she had to stay home and do housework. Whenever she complained to her brothers, her mother would say, "Ella Mae, stop fussing!" I am pretty sure this is why she doesn't let us do anything alone, even to this day. She believes in being equitable; everyone should carry his or her own weight. Even today, I have to make my mom sit down and rest when she visits my home.

My mom always created an environment of openness in our home; we could talk about anything. Nothing was ever off limits. NOTHING! A constant theme for her pep talks was "men" and how, if given the chance, they could take advantage of young girls. She told us of her experience with and older man who frequented the liquor house operated in her parent's home. She said he would come over, look at her in a creepy way, and say he was going to marry her and she hated it. So, she tried to avoid him at all cost. But for some reason on this particular day, she found herself in the same room with him and while her father stepped into the kitchen to go prepare his drink. The creepy old man starts again to say, he was going to marry her. My mom said that she became infuriated and felt so violated by this old man's disgusting proposal that she spit in his face, drawing mucous from the deep recesses of her belly, replete with snorting sounds. She is satisfied. He gets the message and doesn't bother her again.

Maybe this is why she has always taught us, her daughters, that woman must carry themselves differently. She cautioned us or rather prohibited us from sitting in a man's lap, and warned us not be the loudest girl in the room, and "Get somewhere and sit down!" Through her experiences, she has learned that some men, if driven by desire alone, have the capability of making really bad choices. However, women, can dissuade the outcome by avoiding certain situations altogether.

My mother is by nature "The fixer." She can look at a plant and immediately break off what is brown, cut off the withered pieces if needed, place a support beam inside the pot and tie the plant to it so that it will straighten and correct itself. There is a nurturer in her that says everything can change with time, patience, love and attention. A common theme, "Hope always wins" seemed to play itself over and over again in her life.

For example, my grandfather, who was abusive to my grandmother for many years, eventually became a born again Christian. He was never the same again. The loving father image and the image of the husband became one. As a result, for many of his grandchildren, including me, our earliest memories of my grandfather are of an endearing grandfather who played checkers well, loved fish fries, watermelon and laughed a lot. My grandmother remained with my grandfather until his passing.

Now don't it twisted, my mom didn't see life through rose-colored glasses. On the contrary, she has perfect vision, twenty/twenty to be exact. She is able to see things for what they are and still be accepting. She understands that every individual has imperfections and flaws but their core desire is to do well, be better; that is why we all need Jesus. I'm a lot like my mother. I understand that everyone is flawed but we all can change.

————

Many years later, my grandfather would pass away and my grandmother emerges as the central figure or the "Grand Dame" of my mom's family. I was so young when my grandfather was alive that I don't have a lot of memories of him. I do remember watching captivated by the many tricks and illusions my grandfather would perform using only a piece of twine and cardboard. I don't remember us talking much, I would just stand and watch for a while, then go and grab one of the homemade sausage or ham biscuits grandma would have resting on the potbelly stove, as I ran through the kitchen on my way back outside to play "Genie" in the sand. It seemed like every weekend we were together. There was always a lot of laughter at the house during those days.

After my granddaddy, passed, my grandma became more visible to me for some reason. I began to notice her, full of passion, and flair. I noticed her grace, audacity and style. She loved wearing nice clothes and "high" heels, which were my favorite. My grandma became my style icon. She looked good in her clothes too, which made many a man take notice. I admired her bravado and her finesse because contrarily, her daughter, my mom, was very moderate and understated. My grandmother's style gave me something to aim for. When I was older, my mom told me that my grandmother's fire and passion made her very attractive. I'll just say, she didn't have trouble having her needs met. That explains how when granddaddy passed, Mr. Jimmy was waiting in the wings to pick up the pieces. Ironically, no one spoke a coarse word to say about it to her or him. My guess is that they calculated that because she had endured so much in her earlier years that she should be able to enjoy some moments of pleasure.

All of these experiences had a profound effect on my mother's parenting ideologies. It would be virtually impossible for anyone to live through any of this and not come out without making some life altering decisions. Could this is the reason why my mom stayed with my dad? Maybe she resolved a long time ago that things would get better with love and nurturing. Oh yeah, my father, also lived through many heartbreaking life situations could make it appear as if the deck is stacked against him. How could he make a marriage work? He had never seen it done before.

My dad was a functioning, fully employed alcoholic. I remember as a child about four or five years old, my dad would get drunk, he would start to shadow box. One particular night, he jabbing at the air very close to my mom's face, but she does not flinch. I guess growing up with six brothers, living with her dad, and watching her mother live through domestic violence, my mom knew all too well, where this behavior could only lead. This was a familiar place. However, having different options available, she decided to make a different decision. She quietly stands up, walks into the kitchen, and returns with a cast iron skillet. She calmly, but firmly tells my dad that if he ever hits her, she would be forced to fight but she would not fight fair. She said she would pick up whatever she could and use it!

Wow! My dad continues to drink but the shadow boxing ceases forever that night.

I'm sure the thoughts of having to stand up for her little brother, the old man who harassed her and what her mother endured, all flashed before her eyes. That was the first and the last time my dad ever did this. My dad also understood that this was not your average woman. She didn't need protecting. She could protect herself and she was women enough to allow herself to be protected.

My mother always had a clear understanding of how the family dynamic should work. She cooked meals for my dad and set the table. We would wait until his plate was made before we could start eating. She didn't have to do it but something inside my mother understood the power of honor and order. She honored my father, not just for who he was, but for the position he held in the home. Everyone knew his or her role in the family dynamic. We each were called to hold up our part of the family order. She expected it. The family dynamic was what gave my mother and father a shared sense of "I'm doing something right." My mother would often have to uphold this standard alone, and God has honored her for it.

I remember when my mother became a born again Christian. It was a complete 180-degree change. Instantly, the music changed from Earth Wind and Fire to WPJL, the only local Christian Radio station at the time. It was then that I began to see the love and healing flow from God's heart to my mom's. Many times I would walk into the kitchen only to find my mom on the floor in tears worshipping the Father. I knew then that God was real! My dad also knew something had changed, my mom no longer wanted to drink beer or go out. She would choose instead to attend Bible Study and Sunday school. She would even hold Bible study or family devotion in our home.

Trying to deflect our attention, my dad would grunt, complain or try to make us laugh while my mom was teaching or praying, but she didn't waiver. She understood that she had to be the spiritual leader at that time, and she made it her responsibility to make it happen. Mom would weekly call us all together to pray and quote scriptures for Bible Study. Even though we laughed and joked a lot during these times, we really enjoyed this time and knew it really was a serious a reverent time. What we were unaware of was that the seed of the word was being planted, watered and the stakes secured in our hearts.

When I experienced my very first heartbreak, I recalled my mother on her knees in the kitchen, her tears and her transformation. I knew as if it was calling from dep within me what I was supposed to do. I asked my mother to pray with me and lead me in "The Sinner's Prayer." It was for me, one of the sweetest moments in my life. I am however, the oldest of four, so I cannot completely draw a picture of the matriarch, my mother without including my siblings and their viewpoints. To attempt to do so would create a misleading, one-dimensional image at best. LOL...Even Jesus had four different viewpoints to articulate his deity.

———

This is what my "baby" sister had to say:

Shae: *Initially I was a little apprehensive when my sister asked me to write something about our mother. I mean she can't be summed up into one paragraph! She is an outstanding mother, but that is what most people can say about their mom. However, this is my real perception.*

"...my mom is outstanding because she taught us a plethora of things that she learned over her life time. She taught me how to cook, clean, parent, be kind, etc. The one lesson that stood out the most, for me, was that "Love Hurts!" She told me that having sex with the right person was amazing, full of enjoyment and pleasure. However, there is another side which could lead you through unnecessary pain physically and

emotionally. She gave scenarios like you (would) give yourself to someone and they left you the next day high and dry. Maybe they told you they loved you only to satisfy their thrills, but really, they didn't care two cents about you. This lesson stuck with me and I was a virgin until Mr. Right found me because I didn't just want to be anyone's cheap thrill! Again, this is just one lesson out of many, and I hope it blesses someone as it has blessed me.

In conclusion, I am only one of four, but today my mom can say that all of her children, Tonya, Shae and Al have grown to know and love the Lord. Are we perfect? No! But, we're forgiven! What a testimony!

VILLAGE SANCTUARY

I remember riding the school bus to the elementary school one day. I was the new kid. I was somewhat shy and quiet and kept to myself. All I had known was the comforts of home. One day I had to ride in the back of the bus and there was a lot going on in the back of the bus. Older boys and girls were kissing and "being fast". Which is what my mom would call it. Then for no apparent reason, one of the popular boys sitting near me in the back of the bus starts saying something about me. I don't recall what he was saying but I do remember wanting to shrink away and hurry off the bus at my stop. All of a sudden, things take a turn for the worse!

This boy spits in my hair! Ugh! I remember the cold, wetness on top of my head and my fingers touching the gooey, sticky, slimy mucous pooling on top of my newly pressed hair. I remember this almost as if it were yesterday. Then all of a sudden, like a super heroes, two "Fast girls" jump to my rescue! They tell him he was wrong and shouldn't have done that, while the older of the two, wipes my hair as if she was mothering me. The younger one, who turns out to be her cousin, threatened to beat him up if he ever tried to do anything like that again. Guess what? He didn't.

These two cousins, Priscilla and Tracy, became my friends and bodyguards. From that day forward, I felt as if some of their "girl power" transferred to me; I felt untouchable!

I went from being the "new girl" alone to a girl with friends, powerful ones at that. Funny thing is though, I never went to their house and they would always come to mine.

I had vinyl records that would play (records? I know... A long time ago, right?) read-along-books. It would be stories like "Rumpelstiltskin", the "Three Billy Goats Gruff", and other fairy tales. These so-called "Fast girls" would come to my house, lay on the floor beside me, and listen to the stories. This went on for years until they went to middle school. Later on, I understood that they had unhealthy home environments and silently endured much and my home allowed them some respite; for these girls, it had become the Village Sanctuary. They would not the only ones....

The matriarch also mothers the community or the village. Many of my friends would come to our house after school and on weekends and I would go to theirs, if my mother approved. Well, if you came anywhere near a good mother you know she would treat you as if you were "her own". If you could not abide by her rules and that understanding then you might as well go home! One of my dearest childhood friends shares here recollection of her interaction with my mother:

DeAngela: *I imagine that we have all had "that one friend" encounter in our lives. "That one friend" was the one upon whom you could always rely to lighten the load through effortlessly became part of their circle. My one friend in through the thin. She shared her family with you and you shared her Montague Family with me.*

Mrs. Ella, Alnita's mom, made such a lasting impression on me in those really awkward teenage years. She embraced many with whom she came in contact, and treated no one different. She would tell you the truth even when her honesty cut like a blade...for it was the medicated (loving) clean-up that made her words of truth more bearable in the end. There was no question that Jesus was the One she served faithfully, and you didn't enter or leave her house without a golden nugget of wisdom. There were words of discipline that you knew you were going to hear before you stepped foot over the threshold, especially when you knew you were wrong. I remember the day I wore a pair of shorts significantly shorter than my norm and I thought I was cute. In fact, no one could tell me anything different...except Mrs. Ella. She looked at me when I came through the door and said something like, "Now, do you really think those shorts are becoming of a young woman? You don't need to be showing these boys your secrets." The very next few sentences were of us as young women carrying ourselves with respect the way God would have it and reinforcing the fact that she loved us and wanted to see us do well.

I loved Mrs. Montague's cooking! She always had something delicious to eat when I visited, which was practically every day. I remember the leftovers even being scrumptious because there were plenty of them that I ate from her table. Breakfast was never complete without her sausage and eggs with cheese. Alnita and I took turns eating at each other's home, but I seemed to visit the Montague home much more frequently, by choice. It wasn't long before I became a mainstay at the Montague home.

I adored my visits and often hated to leave. It was difficult to put my finger on it at the time, but I've had an opportunity to reflect and experience the nostalgia of walking up the hill and around the corner to the Montague house. I now know that it was the love of Jesus and warmth of His spirit that made me feel so delightful and kept me coming back. I'm so thankful for "that one friend" experience! Most importantly, I am eternally grateful that Mrs. Ella was the servant God chose to show me all about His unconditional love. The greatest memory of all about Mrs. Ella? She loved tirelessly with a servant's heart!

———

It truly does take a village. I knew I was going to get the same type of nurturing at DeAngela's house as well. This wasn't an anomaly during our times and in our community. This type of

Matriarch often lived next door. Our neighbors took care of each other's children; they shared the responsibility of keeping a close eye on all the children. You could not do wrong and go unnoticed. This modern day mantra "snitches get stitches" did not exist. For us it meant the exact opposite, "Snitches get switches!"

The Elder Women should teach the Younger...

Last but definitely not least, the bible states in I Corinthians 7:14 (NIV),*"for the Christian wife brings holiness to her marriage... Otherwise, your children, would not be holy, but now they are holy."*

Hallelujah! Because of her love for the Father and faith in His word, my mother, has allowed her life to become a conduit for His grace and mercy to flow, changing forever our generations.

All the hurt, disappointment and pain of the past have all been washed away. My sisters and brother, my children, my nephews and nieces have a good understanding of whom Jesus is and how He makes life so much sweeter because of my mom's faithfulness Sure, we experience life situations, but we do not have to wonder where God is in all of it.

My mother taught us how to pray, read the Bible and believe God. We can truly say we have a generation of Believers. What an amazing legacy!

So the seeds have been planted, the plants have been pruned and all the withered edges cut away. He is the Vine and we are the branches. We abide in Him and He in us. We are one with Him and we know it. All because a little girl, dared to see people for who they are and love them anyway, flaws and all.

So now, it's my turn!

ALICE GARRETT: THE GREATEST MOM OF ALL

Ella Mae Montague

I can't begin to tell you how sweet my mother, Alice Lennell Allen Garrett, was. In my eyes, she was the greatest "lady on the planet." She stayed at home and made sure that my family had what we needed. From the time I could remember she provided the things I needed since I was the only girl. She taught me the right way to do things, even as a young child. I wasn't perfect, but because she would constantly let me know to "act as good as I looked." I tried to do just that.

My mom was the kind of mother who worked hard to provide for me and my six brothers. She made sure we were clean and dressed right before we left home. She made sure we had 25 cents for our lunch everyday, which now doesn't seem like much, but during those days it meant hard work. She had to work hard to provide for us all the equally. My mom believed in doing fairly; she wanted to do what was right and proper. Watching my mother take care of her own grandchildren is what encouraged me to become a small business owner and open a Daycare. She was a shining example of strength and courage to me.

I am the only living daughter. My mom gave birth to a little girl who would have been 9 years older than me, but she lived for only three months. My mom never spoke about her death to me, but I've always longed for a sister. Being the fifth of seven children, the only girl and born prematurely, made me have to fight from the beginning. My mom says they had to cut my hair because it was so long that it was draining my strength. Maybe that's why I've always had that fight in me. I had to fight from the beginning.

Oh, my mother was a great cook! She knew how to stretch a little bit of food and make a feast fit to feed our big family. She also knew how to cook a variety of different items, many different ways. No matter what she cooked it...

IT WAS ALWAYS DELICIOUS!

During the summer, she would do her canning, so that in the winter we would have food stored up. This was wise because during the winter it was especially hard for us. Our friends were always looking for excuses to come over to the house. My six brother's friends, especially, loved to come over just to eat my mother's cooking. She was known around town for her cooking. She made the best pies and cakes, homemade banana pudding, sweet potato "Jacks', which is a sweet potato turnover. She also made potato cakes, which are like hash browns. Her biscuits and gravy, fried chicken were also the best!

My mother, she would work many different jobs. She was known in our small town of Varina, for her cooking but she would also work in grocery stores, restaurants, cooking and running the store. She would also clean houses, iron clothes, and fold bed sheets so that they had no wrinkles. My mom hired herself out to an older white woman who knew how to sew. She cleaned the woman's house and ironed clothing. My mom would get this person to sew dresses for me, so my clothing was "one-of-kind". They were all beautiful and unique which made me feel so special because my mother would have this done just for me. The person didn't charge my mother a lot for this either, probably because my mother was such a good worker. And now, that I understand

God's love and mercy, it was the goodness of God. My mother always wanted me to look and be my best at all times! God provided a way for this to happen with ease. I would also get her daughter's clothes when they were too little for her. My mother also always made sure my hair was looking "good." She wanted me to feel good about myself. She also made sure she kept herself looking good, too...

She never told me that I was pretty, though. She would say, "Act as good as you look and you'll be fine." This didn't bother me because I knew that she loved me. I believe she told me this because she didn't want me to get "big headed." However, much later in life, my brothers shared with me that they heard that my mother was very attractive as a young woman. I'm not sure what issues that may have caused her, but she made sure that I was level-headed and avoided those issues as much as possible.

Nevertheless, I loved that my mom and I could talk about anything. She was a stay-at-home mom and that made me feel secure. If she went anywhere, she would make sure my brothers were home with me until she returned. She loved the boys just as much as she loved me, but she knew they could pretty much take care of themselves.

Since I was the only girl, she had to teach me how to cook. She started when I was about 11 or 12. My daddy eat my food and tell me my food was good even if it really wasn't. He was nice to me, but he was not always nice to my mother. This was very clear. My mom married my dad when she was 14 and my father was 21. She had never been away from home and had to learn to stay with my father in order to raise her siblings, and now her seven children. Some of the things she took and had to deal with showed me an example of a strong woman. She stayed and endured a marriage with my father nearly 60 years. But despite how he treated my mother, I loved my father also and out of all of his siblings, he was the only one who remained in his first marriage. They somehow kept our family together.

Although they had some difficult situations, they showed me that as a wife and as a parent I could do the same. My mom chose to stay and fight it out spiritually because she knew we needed them to stay together. God instilled this in my father also near the end.

In my own marriage of forty-five plus years, I thank God, that I've had this example. Because my mom showed me her example, I know I can do it and now even better! It is now my hope that my children are able to do even better for their children. My prayer is that they are able to love themselves and love their children, down the line and for many generations as much or greater as my mom loved me.

WISDOM, LOVE AND LAUGHTER

Dorothy Montague Foster

Oteria Watson Montague: a woman of determination with a keen sense of survival. Mother endured the struggles of raising five children, basically alone, all of whom have successfully navigated life utilizing the skills and knowledge she instilled in us. Her sense of humor would light up the room when she entered. She had self confidence that exploded when there was a need to provide for her children. Oteria Watson Montague was a true believer in her spirituality as it pertains to her salvation.

Mother had the innate ability to discern the value of humor and fun and its healing effect. Her jokes and imaginary tall-tales kept hope alive in her children. Mother's fantasy meals, as imaginary as they were, made us forget the hunger pains. Those were the times that we became stronger as individuals and we could stand and be proud.

She opened our eyes to the inequities of the world and as a result, we are still standing strong and proud. Standing with visions of imaginary ham biscuits and chicken bone soup.

My grandmother is the person you would never forget. Her personality was electric and would light up the room. You couldn't be around her and be down for long; her humor was infectious. If you sat with her for a few moments you would feel the warmth of her smile, and then give it a few minutes tears of laughter would eventually start rolling down your cheeks because she was hilarious. She was warm and caring, mixed with a bit of daring. She was one of the sharpest dressing women I knew but she would also walk outside in nothing but her long-line bra and her slip on given the right situation. She would do anything for a laugh.

It was this ability to make people laugh that my dad said would take their mind off the very real fact they were actually hungry. She would ask them to use their imagination and create what they wanted to eat. Maybe this is why all four of her children are successful to this day. The taught them the power of their creative power. She may not have even understood it but it worked.

Grandma T, is what I called her, was fierce. She had a few choice words she could use to express herself oh so well with. I remember once when we were at church eating cupcakes at a repast. She accidentally dropped it in the grass. Before you know it, she burst out with one of her favorite expletives, "Sugar-Honey-Ice-Tea!" She doesn't even bat an eye that this just happened at church. All of the grandchildren standing near grandma are laughing hysterically. We are literally in tears.

She was brave. She didn't have the best husband and but she was brave enough to walk away. She rode the city bus system daily to and from work all while living alone. She experienced the tragic loss of her son by drowning and much more but she was always smiling. Grandma T taught me how to wear makeup because she was a loyal "Fashion Fair" brand ambassador. She would encourage me to put some rouge on, but still keep on my ruffled socks, what an oxymoron.

Oh, to be able to go to Grandma T's house again, and lay on her bed during the middle of the day! She would let you rest quietly until the exact time you asked to be awakened. Her house was the perfect temperature and the bed was just right. You could feel her put a blanket over you while you lay there. This was utopia.

I asked my dad, Al Jolson Montague, the oldest son, to talk about his mother. This is what he said:

She taught me so many things! Like how to survive as the head of your house. She told me to not let my children experience hard times like I did. She told me to never leave my family. Make sure your family is taken care of before you think about another person (woman) especially being the man of the house. She said I was the protector of the family and that it was my responsibility to take care of my wife and children. She always made you laugh! But, she would always say real serious quips and quotes that would make you think. Things like, "life is real, life is honest, Life is but an empty dream" (Side note: This is a quote from a Henry

Wadsworth Longfellow poem A Psalm of Life)

Go figure, my grandma T is quoting Henry Wadsworth Longfellow. Wow!

HOW TO MAKE YOUR HOME IN A DUSTY OLD HOUSE

Carlene Hill Byron

My mother grew up on a Maine farm where dirt was what made plants grow. I imagine her mother taught her something about cleaning. Otherwise, the farmhouse kitchen linoleum would never have been a place for me to be seated in my toddler overalls, a box with muffin crumbs between my chubby, outstretched legs and a chicken in my lap, waving one finger at Dad's camera as if I was practicing preaching. Still, cleaning was never high on Mom's list of priorities.

One of my vivid childhood memories is of Mom standing on a scaffold, six or eight feet off the ground, holding a wooden clapboard in place as Dad nailed new siding on the back of our house. I remember vividly another day before we owned a house. Six of us lived in a cramped single-wide near the military base where Dad worked. At the moment I recall, Mom was wrapped in her apron of the era: cream, patterned with tiny men and women formed of yellow and black triangles, almost certainly hand-sewn. The four children, all aged six and under, were playing in the "dining area" while she worked. She turned toward us, lifting from the oven a pan of hot, freshly baked cream puffs. She set the pastries on top of the range to cool, then began pulling out milk and eggs for a from-scratch vanilla custard filling.

Who bakes cream puffs with four little children crowding her feet?

It could be a woman driven by her generation's version of Pinterest shaming. Cream puffs are listed among "50 Basic Recipes for Beginners" in that era's Fannie Farmer *Boston Cooking-School Cookbook*. (Other "basic recipes" included mayonnaise, fruit jam, doughnuts, chicken timbales, and "Canning Fruits and Vegetables.") But my mother's intense engagement with the kitchen could also represent the drive of a woman who took great joy in her own competence. I tend to think that my capable mother took the Fannie Farmer list as a challenge that she expected to master, easily and with pleasure.

Mom mastered many challenges during my childhood. Raising five children to capable adulthood is challenge enough for many. Doing it within a tightly constrained income, so that "shopping" was mostly done at the Navy Relief thrift store, was another. Still another challenge was renovating the old farmhouse we bought, that came with knob and tube wiring, an antique coal furnace, and a kitchen whose "upgrades" to date mostly consisted of replacing the 1913 hand pump with running water.

I don't remember Mom falling under her burdens. I remember her pressing into a blackberry thicket to collect colander after colander of fat, finger-staining fruit. I remember her peeling and slicing entire sacks of fall apples to cook into applesauce that we ate warm with vanilla ice before she packed the rest into the freezer. I remember how hot brown molasses would billow and foam when she added baking soda, just before stirring the sloppy mess into a giant vat of popped corn for holiday cornballs. I remember Mom leading her five little ducklings on summer bicycle rides down country roads, and I can imagine her sitting beside the farm pond of her childhood home as we swam and rowed and capsized the unfortunate "boats" we built ourselves. I remember her fingers endlessly knitting yarn into hats and mittens – first for all of us, then for local charities.

I have almost no memory of Mom with mop or dust rag or vacuum cleaner in hand. I can't remember Mom polishing furniture. I can see her cleaning up thrift store furniture finds and repainting them. I can remember the formula for her home brewed paint stripper. But I can't see her dusting. She must have cleaned floors, especially during the early spring weeks that we in Maine call "mud season." I just can't recall it.

Nor can I recall any significant lessons about housekeeping at her hands. When I was a young bride, I purchased a couple of paperback books that taught me how to clean my house. A little later, I subscribed to a website that encouraged me to create at least one small vision of order in my generally chaotic home. That wasn't a new idea to me. Mom and I both had our little ordered visions. We both created 3D still life arrangements on mantels and in china cabinets and on bookshelves and on side tables. We hung our arranged histories on the walls of our homes. Neither of us looked past those lovely spots and imagined our homes "chaotic." We both thought of our homes as "busy" places where "creative" people had "projects underway." As for the floors... of course the place you walk gets dirty!

But during the years when my sisters and I were young single women sharing apartments with other young single women, each of us stumbled across a startling revelation. One day in each of our lives, after living with women who knew how to keep house, each of us returned to our mother's home and discovered a thin gray film we'd never seen. Our house, we realized, was unkempt. We each remarked to ourselves:

"This house is dusty!"

Each, on her own day, grabbed a rag and a vacuum and sought to correct the failings of the family home. Each returned to her own adult home and either trained herself in the habits of our time's hygienic housekeeping or relapsed into the busy, disordered—even dirty—way of life we learned at our mother's knee.

There are no "dust bunnies" in my home today. Dust gathers itself into ferocious gray wolves, trumpeting elephants, and charging rhinoceroses, ready to burst from the caverns they've found under furnishings and thunder across the savanna of my floors. Accumulated neglect would like to overpower my day, my time, my mind. "Dirty!" it roars. "Unsanitary!" it shouts. It bellows at the last, "Bad housekeeper!"

Like a powerful incantation, a single sentence from memory holds back the hostile judgments. The words come in my mother's voice, issuing from under merry brown eyes: *"If your floor's not clean enough to eat off, don't eat off it."*

I won't, Mom. I promise.

Today, instead of trying to eat off my floor, I'll probably bake something yummy. I'll finish sewing curtains for the dining room and repairing the side table that has loose joints. I might break up the ice that slicks the driveway or make soup from the bone broth that has chilled to gelatin in the refrigerator.

After all of that, I could decide to hunt a dusty gray elephant or a rhinoceros. But probably not. I don't plan to let beasts made from dead dust eat up my life. I plan to consume my own life, nourished by what gives me joy, unafraid of the kinds of wild things that dissolve into clouds at each footfall.

You can keep a house or you can make a home. Mom taught me which was most important.

MOM'S ADVICE

Dr. Diane Suber

When you're a teenager, and even into those middle years of 35-ish, when you think you're living a "grown-up" life – but not really -ANY and EVERYTHING that shakes the balance in your life is a calamity. You pay off the car you bought right after graduating from college and a part that is NOT under warranty suddenly breaks and needs to be replaced. You find the perfect apartment but soon realize that you are short of the first and last month's rent necessary to sign the lease. You take the job that your parents advised was probably not the right fit for you, and within months, you're "released" from the company.

My dad always knew how to help us fix things. Whenever we were in real trouble, we always called my dad. Mom used to say that she always knew something was serious when she answered the phone and we immediately asked her "Is Daddy there?" even before asking how she was doing.

As I look back from this vantage point of 60 years old and counting, I know it wasn't that we loved Daddy more, or thought he was smarter than Mom. It was more that Daddy had a system of analyzing a problem, helping you lay out all the possible scenarios, and determining a plan of action which he would oversee until the problem was resolved. He never seemed to be stumped or unable to work "our" way out of a situation.

Mom? Well, as far back as I can remember Mom's advice for addressing any dilemma—no matter how many moving parts there were or how critical the issue appeared to be, Mom's advice was to: *"Go in and take a hot bath; and then lie down across the bed."* Somehow, at 10 years old, or 16 years old or 25 years old or, even at 36 years old, that advice just seemed to be too nurturing – too maternal—too cliché to be effective.

But today, now that I have become my mother, having raised two children of my own, I look back over my life, and the trials, tribulations, challenges, and mountains that I have faced—and mastered—and I understand that Mom's advice of *"Go in and take a hot bath and lie down across the bed* makes perfect sense and is dead on point. And as I sort through the many life experiences through which I've journeyed, I've come to realize that, whenever, at the very moment that I took Mom's advice, I was able to take control of the situation and restore balance to my life.

You see, all too often we overreact to situations that jar life's balance. We see disaster where there is only turbulence. We see fatalistic outcomes when the facts would bear out alternative endings. We panic and we respond to factors that may be temporary or distorted, or miscues based on the perceptions of others. We may be short-sighted or be hampered by the limitations of our own experiences. We fail to look around the corner or project beyond the "happening right now or in the moment" event.

BUT . . .

As soon as I turn on the water and run my hand under the faucet to test for the temperature and hear the rush of the water filling that tub, I feel comforted. When I undress and step into that tub of hot water, I sense the immediacy of my muscles relaxing and the release the tensions and the stress that are holding me hostage. And in the briefest of moments, those crippling emotions and fears and anxieties that have overwhelmed me start to subside. The calmness of the hot water is contagious and I can feel my body slowly let loose of the thoughts and feelings that hold me captive. If I close my eyes I envision the times of happiness and joy that I've known over the years. I think of the people who have made a difference in my life and I remember the special lessons that I've learned from these people—lessons that made me strong and smart and confident. I can feel the touch of my mother's hand as when she used to brush and braid my hair; and I can hear the lilt and the rhythm in her voice as she read out loud the stories and nursery rhymes I loved. I close my eyes and I see my Mom holding my first child—her first grandchild—and I am comforted by the memory of the love she had for my dad.

I smile. . .

And when I dry myself off, I laugh at the thought of her teaching us how to correctly fold a towel and how to make the hospital corners that hold, in place, the sheets on a freshly made bed. I remember how much she loved playing pinochle and what an incredibly talented tailor she was.

She told me once that, "Whenever you quit a boy, let him think it's because you just don't think you're the right person for him; or because your parents don't want you to have a boyfriend" (I must have been about 12 years old when she told me that). "That way," she said, "the boy won't be angry with you and you can still be friends." Funny, that advice, worked for a long time—way pass 12 years old!

And then I lay down across the bed and I begin to see the real ins and outs of the problem I face. I am calm and assured and comfortable with my ability to find a workable solution. I lay quietly for a while. Maybe I even drift off to sleep for a short nap. But then I get up; get a pad and pen; and make notes. I look at the best possible scenario and the worst ever scenario and I realize that the issues are not as grave as they once seemed and that there are, maybe, several options I might consider that will resolve the issue or, simply, just make the mess go away!

Whether I resolve every issue or not, it has become apparent through the years, that Mom's advice is so much more powerful than the actual words would suggest. In a moment when the world seems to have thrown me a sucker punch, Mom's advice gives me back the power of me over me. It restores balance. It neutralizes polarizing forces and opens up real possibilities.

"Go in and take a hot bath and then lie down across the bed."

Thanks, Mom. . .

MOM, DID YOU KNOW?

DeAngela Perry

PURPOSE

You gave life to a 1-month premature, 3-lb baby girl in 1971. Did you know that baby would turn out to be a worshipper... a praiser... a Kingdom-thinker and builder? That little miracle baby has purpose!

PRAISE

You expressed your pride in that little girl for so many years, through cute clothes and shoes fit for a queen, adorable bows, sweet words of affirmation, and the warm touch of a mother's hand. WOW! Were you aware that your little Queen Victorian angel would be so confident in herself, so poised in her speech, so prideful in her countenance, and so loving of her relationship with our Father in Heaven? It was all because of what you said, what you did, and how you carried yourself.

PRACTICALITY

I'm sure you never dreamed that your baby girl would turn into a woman who practices order and organization, makes great use of skills, and believes in dependability. Undoubtedly, your experience in the US Army prepared you to utilize those same skills at home. It was all because of the precedent you set in school, on your jobs, and in your home. We were so much alike, always wanting to ensure anyone and everyone with whom we came in contact left our presence with a feeling of sincere warmth and care that only we could give in our very own way. You raised a steady compliant, full of compassion and love.

EXCITABLY HUMOROUS

What about those many heated rival basketball games we watched between the NC State Wolfpack and UNC Tarheels, laughing at each other one moment and on the edge of our seats the next, with great anticipation that my team would beat your team and we would "shake on it" in the end and say "good job." Did you ever believe that your sweet-sixteener would turn into a relatively noncompetitive adult with lots of passion for fun and laughing out loud? Well, ask my co-workers... they hear me EVERY DAY!

EAGER TO LEARN

Remember when I sat behind you many times at home, while you effortlessly typed 90 words per minute, thinking that ever becoming that efficient was a far-fetched dream? Remember the many days you pushed me to practice until I finally got it? You probably never dreamed that your often-frustrated teenager would transform into a woman always wanting to learn more, be more, and most importantly, give more!

Well, I'm here to tell you mom that I am who I am because of who you were. I wore your patience thin many days and nights, but you still found a way to show me love. I hated the disciplinarian in you because your punishments always seemed so harsh, but I thank you for them today because I am able to establish boundaries and tolerance in many situations. You were such an awesome chef and I stared in amazement at your talents.... and I am happy to say that I am actively seeking to make you proud in that very delicate, underdeveloped arena known as the kitchen. Still pressin' in that area, mom... still pressin'!

I guess what I really needed you to know is when you thought I wasn't listening, I was. When you thought I didn't care, I did. When you guessed I would turn out to be something great, your guess was correct! I am great in God! Through your example, I have learned the dos and the don'ts, the rights and the wrongs, the yes's and the no's.

I'm sure you never imagined that December 16, 2007 would be your last day on this earth.

Picture, if you will, the day of seeing you after 2 years is suddenly on the horizon: the two-way conversations had taken place, the two-way excitement was building with anticipation of spending quality time together, and the arrangements had been made. I anxiously awaited the phone call you with your words, "I'm here at the airport and checking in my luggage", that phone call that never happened. You were so excited to be coming home to meet your then-14-month-old grandson for the first time and seeing your 9-yr-old granddaughter after 2 years, the visit home that never happened.

My heart was heavily hurting while all of the "wish I could have" thoughts had been running through my mind. I never had an opportunity to say goodbye, a tough and unplanned transition that happened unbeknownst to me. However, my spirit yet rejoices today knowing that God receives the glory. He's so faithful because He allows me to press through my pain to pour into my friends and loved ones. Guess what? You did the very same when your circle of friends were experiencing their storms. I remember you sitting at the kitchen table encouraging others and you were experiencing distress in your own life---WOW! You didn't even know all the power you had when you bore that 3-lb baby girl. Thank you, Mom for loving me enough to be loved by me. I share this tribute from my heart to yours....

Hey ma, how ya' doing?" was the start of many chats.
I was always so proud of you, for you wore many of life's hats....
From businesswoman by day to chef and mom at
night, You never missed a one-time chance to
spread your beautiful light.
I never knew what hunger was or how to live without,
You taught me truth and morals, and what life was all about.
I learned from your independence and taking care of me,
Neatness and order followed our names, as anyone could see.
I remember the infectious laughs and times we spent together
with such big dreams and excitement
of "us" getting better and better.
Although I can no longer see your smiling face,
Through tears of missing you so much, I'll continue to run this race.
Rest assured, ma, you're in our hearts forever,
I'll not forget what you instilled, I promise you, not ever.
As I strive to reach my goals, and always do my part,
I love you and promise to live for God,
with you nestled in my heart.

Love, DeAngela

THINGS I LEARNED FROM MY MOTHER

Peggy Tatum

I was fortunate enough to have my mother all my life until recently. She died at the age of 90 after whispering a prayer one morning. So for 60 years, I was always her child and never seemed to grow up. She always had these sayings that you really didn't understand until later in life when the light bulb came on.

"There is more to taking care of than having." As a little girl that meant absolutely nothing other than I just did something wrong and missed getting a whipping. I learned from my mom that even though a whipping with a switch hurt and messed up my legs, it was a deterrent from getting into trouble. My younger brother didn't seem to get it and he got whippings long after me. Mom would say, "You're a big cigar, but I can still smoke you!" After my brother reached 6 feet, he grabbed mom by the arms one day and just held on to her. He was tired of getting whippings and it was tiring her out whipping him so they called a truce. She wasn't abusive in any manner, but she worked too hard to provide for us and we not honor or obey her. She was the disciplinarian while my father kept his cool. The six of us turned out pretty good with no dysfunctions.

Mom taught us to stick together. She did it by example when

she married at 15 and birthed 7 kids with one dying at two years old. This was done at a time when women had children and gave them away to be raised by someone else when they couldn't afford to or just wasn't ready to raise a family. She along with my father provided for us as best they could. She knew how to make food from scraps and leftovers in the field. Dad would set a rabbit trap and yes, like Daniel Boone, we ate wild game. I remember the meat that hung in the smoke house that got too old and was passed along to us from Mr. Lin where we were tenant farmers. We never got the good stuff – even the pecans were rank when they were passed along. Mom had a way of sanitizing, cooking and making some red eye gravy in her skillet. We didn't have anything to compare it to, so to us, everything was good. Those skills were not passed on to me. I was the last girl to leave home and mom wasn't fond of the dishes I learned to make in Home Economics class so she opted to do all the cooking. Lucky for me, I married a man who could cook.

Mom taught me that even though certain folks smile in your face, they don't want you in their kids' lives beyond being their servants. She lived in a different time and experienced many transitions whereas I was a baby boomer and hadn't lived through the hate she had encountered.

One profound thing she taught me goes a long way with church etiquette. When I spoke with her about disagreeing with the pastor's rhetoric, she said that when she disagrees, she just put her attention on God, concentrate on him and praise God, not man. She basically blocked out any foolishness and didn't "run down" or talk about the preacher. She would say, "They got to give an account for themselves".

I learned about the anointing of gospel music by watching my mom sing in the choir. She loved to sing and we spent many Sunday afternoons visiting churches and singing on their gospel programs. There was something about her singing that could move the crowd and change the atmosphere. During the 70's, she was known for singing, "I Thank You Jesus" which was her signature song that she lived by which I am sure attributed to her long life.

Gardening was in her blood. While dad was living, they had as many as three gardens. When you visited during the summer, be prepared to shell peas, snap beans, shuck corn or anything related to the garden harvest. She had a green thumb which equaled plenty whether it was the vegetable or flower garden. The summer before she died, I witnessed her bringing back to life a tomato stem that I was trying to root in water. She put it in a cup with a little dirt and nursed it every day and later transplanted into the ground. It grew to become one of the tallest tomato plants in the garden. Things that most people throw away, she would re-purpose.

She was a great seamstress and taught me how to sew. In her latter days, she would sew in the darkness because she couldn't bare the light on her legs. She made quilts that will be memories for a lifetime and was forever altering her clothes to make them fit as her weight dwindled.

Mom loved to laugh and when she got together with her sisters they spent considerable amount of time laughing. My dad called them The Laughing Sisters. They mostly laughed at each other or their shenanigans. The joy she experienced with her sisters has trickled down to the laughter I share with my sisters. Laughter is good for the soul.

Interest rates really upset my mom. She made sure that she paid her bills on time or early. There was a certain look on her face when she talked about interest. The thought of someone taking extra of her hard earned money just rubbed her wrong. Either she saved her money and paid cash, laid it away or did without until she could afford it. Getting in debt was not her thing.

One of the best lessons I learned from mom was to eat fresh vegetables, fruits and take care of your body and love everybody.

Many of her cures for illness was simple stuff like using Epsom salt, Creomulsion cough syrup, peroxide, alcohol and Vick's Vapor Rub. At her death, she was only on one prescription drug, Lasix.

While I was blessed to have a mother for 60 years, it is my responsibility to continue her legacy of love through my family and share her story. The release of "The Rosie Chronicles" is scheduled for Fall 2017.

I AM MY MOTHER'S DAUGHTER

Shina Miller

I am my Mother's daughter. I grew up an only child and loved every minute of it. I got to have my Mommy all to myself. My Mommy has always been my best friend. Four years ago, my world was completely turned upside down. My Mommy was diagnosed with stage IV thyroid cancer. I've heard so many people say that thyroid cancer is the best cancer to have.... No cancer is the best cancer to have. It is a horrible, terrible disease. The prognosis from the beginning wasn't good due to the metastases to brain, bone and other organs. Based on the doctors, maybe she had a year to a year and a half. But my Mommy never listened to what the doctors said. She always said," I trust God. I'm not going anywhere until He says so." And she carried that for the rest of her life.

Because of her cancer diagnosis, the roles switched and my Mommy was no longer taking care of me but I was taking care of her. I was now being the Mommy. And what a blessing that was!

My Mommy had her thyroid removed, bilateral hip rods placed in each side of her hips due to pathological fractures from the cancer. She even went through different types of brain radiations, gamma knife, cyber knife, and also had 14 rounds of whole brain radiation. Oh, did I fail to mention she did chemo? Never once did she complain or question, why me? She even surprised her doctors at times by how well she was tolerated everything that she had gone through. She remained strong in her faith.

I remember one time she was in the hospital and her sister was crying about what was going on and my Mom looked at her and asked, "Where is your faith?" I am going to be fine.

Everything that she went through, all of the fighting... I knew it was for me. I asked her one day to tell me if she ever got tired. I knew she never would because a mother never wants to see their child hurt. She knew it would hurt me to hear that so she never said it.

My Mommy passed away on Nov. 12th. It's funny how things work out. My Mommy was with me when I took my first breath out of her womb and I was with her when she took her last breath on this earth. She had the biggest smile on her face right before she took her last breath.

From that day, I have never been the same.

I have never experienced such hurt, pain, and devastation.

My heart is broken.

My joy is gone because my purpose is gone.

But even in the midst of all the hurt and pain, I am truly grateful. My Mommy lived for 3 years and 11 months with cancer that most people would not have survived a year with. My Mommy and I always had a close relationship, but her sickness brought us even closer. I had the opportunity to really get to know my Mommy in a way that I never would have. I got to see her at her most vulnerable moments and even in those, she was still encouraging and nurturing me.

My Mommy has always lived her life to the fullest. If she wanted something, regardless of the price, she would get it. If she loved you, she would tell you. If she didn't like something, you would know it. She lived everyday like it would be her last, but she lived it with faith. I was blessed to be able to see this type of living by faith. She had the sweetest soul. I heard her say a couple of months before she went to heaven that either way this ends, if I'm healed on earth or healed in heaven... either way I'm alright.

Since my Mommy's passing I have done a lot of reflecting. I have been asking God a lot of questions like why my Mom?

Why didn't You heal her like I wanted her to be healed? Why would You take my joy and purpose away from me?

Why would You allow me to hurt so much if you love me?

If my Mommy knew that I was doing this she would not be happy with me. She would tell me that God knows the end from the beginning and that God's will is always best. My Mommy always prayed for God's will to be done. She would tell me that God loves me so much that He specifically put certain people in my life that He knew I would need and could help me. She would also say that He loved her so much that He no longer wanted to see her suffering and in pain and although it wasn't the earthly healing that me as her child desired it was the healing that God desired for her. My Mommy was ready to leave this earth far sooner than I was ready for her to leave me. She was ready to rest.

At first I thought that my Mommy taught me everything except for how to live, how to survive, how to push forward without her. But she did teach me those things. She taught me through both her words and actions. She equipped me to be able to do anything I wanted to do and go anywhere that I wanted to go. She taught me that regardless of what is thrown at me in life that all I need to do is trust God. She taught me that if I truly trust God, if I truly give every burden and care to him that He will take care of it. She taught me that no matter what it looks like, no matter what anyone says that as long as I know whose I am that either way it ends, it's alright.

Mommy, I hope I continue to make you proud.

See you later, Sunshine.

A PEONY IS SO HEAVY AND OPEN

Nina Oteria

The peony my mother has cut to
revive me is heavy and open
Smell, she says
Bringing it to my nose
Muse perfume inside the blossom
Returns me heavy and full
I remember her outside the other house
The peonies whose soft layered heads would droop
Weighed with the rain
naturally large and sinking
We used metal spikes to support those
drooped heads leaning,
Ants running over them cause
of the sweetness beside the deck
Beside the raised garden my dad built for me
Where I planted tomatoes on my own
Whose fruits sometimes slumped the vines
Everything down in the dirt brown and weighted
Like that night in 7th grade when I cried and cried

Mixes with the now perfume and my dad laid
on my raised bed to comfort me
Because I was the girl who only wore dresses
And couldn't shut it about God
Alone reverberating in my room
whenever my head drooped
My mom showed me how to tie up
the stalk with a stocking
So the vines could still breathe and the
tomatoes wouldn't rot in standing water
Because they were small
And I grew them in my stockings
How Georgia always put hers on with kid gloves
Head bent to see the toe so they wouldn't run
My mother always smiles when she tells me about it
Her mother would pull the skin tone pair on smooth and
slow before church where I was born again
and again and again
Heavy with perfume and Ms. Clara's red beads
the oil when I smashed my green thumb
Turned it blackblue
Head bent to pray low in the dirt
How to support the neck?
My mother teaches me
"There's no time, so at sunset love
from others can look like one rose."
New syntax speaks with the blossom
trembling with anointing oil
Smell, she says
I rise four inches to linger

Mhm.

Quote from page 22 of Hello, the Roses by Mei-Mei Berssen-Brugge

———

"Is any one among you suffering? Let him pray. Is any cheerful? Let him sing praise. Is any among you sick? Let him call for the elders of the church, and let them pray over him, anointing him with oil in the name of the Lord." James 5:13-14

LIFE IS BEAUTIFUL BECAUSE OF ROSE

Sophia Downing

At age six, I went to court. The judge said "Sophia, take this gavel and with it, show me how bad you want to stay with your mother." I raised the gavel high in the air with both of my hands, and threw it down with all my might. Everyone clapped and laughed. I jumped up and down with excitement. It was a day I will never forget.

My mother overcame a drug addiction and time in jail before she was given full custody of me. I am so thankful to her for choosing motherhood over all else. Safety and unconditional love was a promise my mom made to me when she was given the opportunity to be a parent again.

I'll never forget that for years we did not have our own residence. We often stayed with her friends or at her sister's house. Most of these places were overcrowded. Many nights, my mom's body served as a bed for me. It was her warm chest, or the hard floor. I was unbothered by it. In fact, I loved it because it felt like the safest place in the world.

During those years, my mom attended beauty school and learned how to do hairstyles. She also worked two jobs. They were both maid positions at hotels in the city. I remember having to be at her jobs with her sometimes. I would swim for long hours whenever I was there. Our favorite activity as mother and daughter was swimming. She often rented a room for us so that I could watch cartoons and sleep in a bed sometimes. We didn't have much, but I was a happy child.

Life got better for us after my mom finished beauty school. She reunited with my father and we moved to another state. She found work at a hair salon at the local mall and we finally had our own apartment.

The thing I love most about my mother is her courageous spirit. It took courage to walk away from drugs and a life of crime. It took courage to start over. It took courage to work two to three jobs so that her daughter's needs were met. It took courage to solve the problems my dad, a former drug addict, had often created for us.

I remember one Christmas Eve our home was robbed. It was no coincidence to my mother that the day before, my dad's partners in crime made a visit to our home. While I was at school and she was at work, the thieves entered our home and stole all my Christmas gifts and most of her clothes and shoes. When I arrived home that day, my mom was seated on the porch. It looked like she had been crying for a while. I immediately ran over to her and I asked "mommy, are you alright?" Back then, my mom never talked to me straight. She never wanted me to know the negative things that were happening in our lives. She stood up with a stern face and commanded me to stay out of the house until she came back from running errands. I was eight and could not think of anything more fun than playing outside with my best friends.

While I played outside, my mom was busy riding around to local crack houses and neighborhoods looking for our things. Well, she found them. I don't know all the details, but she returned home with about seventy percent of our possessions. My mother purchased everything she could from a group of strangers.

She never told me exactly what happened. I overheard her telling the facts to her sister over the phone.

As I write these memories on paper, it is evident that my mother cared more about my happiness than her own. She worked night and day, so that we could stay together in our own home. She always taught me to see the good in everyone. I suppose that is why she never talked to me about my dad and his struggles. I found out things mostly by eavesdropping on her phone conversations. She hired the best babysitters for me. My mother always made sure that the babysitter drove me to her job to see her. It was important to her to see me throughout her tiresome day. I knew I was her everything.

Growing up, I witness my mother caring for others for years. I learned how to have a servant's heart from my mother. Cooking was her favorite thing to do for others. During the holidays, she would cook an enormous feast. After the two of us would eat, the remaining food would be packaged and delivered by us to homeless people in the community. Some of the people were drug addicts. I think my mom cared about them because at one point she had walked in their shoes. Also, my dad was somewhere out there too. She also had brothers who wandered the streets, only they were in another state. She did the same for them when she traveled home for the holidays.

The greatest memories I have of my mother were Sunday mornings. The thing I love best was the hearty and country breakfast she made. The thing I dislike most was being sent to church. I was too young to understand the lasting affect it would have on my life and all its benefits. My mother didn't join me most of the time. Sometimes she had to work and at times she just chose not to attend. The funny thing is I always had to go. And I had to ride the church van. I think my mother believed I would learn how to be a good person. I ended up learning so much more. Jesus is the center of my life, and I give my mom some of the credit for that.

Today, at sixty-one, my mother is still the loving and whole-some person she has always been. She still loves me unconditionally and believes that the safest place for me is with her. When I was younger, she demanded that I clean my room and listen to my teachers and do my homework. Today, she demands weekly phone calls, visits, letters, and the greatest gift I could give her, grandkids. While she patiently waits for grandkids, I gladly write the love letters to her on Mother's Day and her birthday. I visit and I call and like most daughters, I'm there for her when she needs me.

MY MOMMY MOMENT

Marilyn Rogers

My proudest moment was becoming a mother in 1979. I had an 8 pound boy named Marreco F. Hackney. He was so beautiful. He had straight hair and when people saw him, they thought he was Hispanic. He had the most beautiful eyes you could ever look into. I remember when he was 8 months old he started teething and his teeth were coming in like wild fire. The fever made him cry something terrible, so I called my grandma who told me to take some potatoes and wrap them around his head and stomach. I said, "Grandma? What is this going to do?" She said it would draw out the fever; and it did. Those potatoes were cooked, I mean they turned so black it was if the fever cooked them. He did not have another fever while he was teething.

Now with my second child, it was different, I had some difficultly with this one. I had some spotting in my 3rd month so I went to the hospital. They told me that I had just had a miscarriage but that I was still pregnant. I was very confused at this time and was not sure what had fully happened. I asked them how I could still be pregnant if I just had a miscarriage. They told me that some women are pregnant with twins and miscarry one, but will still carry the other. This is what seemed to happen to me. I had to deal with the pain of losing a baby and still have another. So in December of 1984, my daughter was born. She was born 8 pounds and 12 ounces just like her big brother. She also was sweet and loveable, to the core. Her grandmother would keep her while I went to work. I would strap her in the bike seat and ride my bike to her grandmother's house and then to work. During this time I was breastfeeding so I pumped and stored my milk. My mother-in-law would store the milk and try to feed my daughter but she didn't like being bottle fed. My daughter would not eat. So my mother-in-law was at a loss. We tried another brand of nipples that felt more real and it worked.

Over the next few years they start to grow up and want more things than I was ever able to give them. My husband picked up the children and told them that they were going to Kings Dominion in Virginia and that his mother was coming. She had never been out of the state so she seemed excited. But on the day we planned to leave, she tried to back out.

We told her, "NO, you have to come!"

When we got on the bus to Virginia, she told us that she was afraid of bridges. We started to laugh. I tried to get her to go to sleep and it worked. She never even knew that she went over the bridges. Well, the kids had a great time. When we returned home, my husband (Fred) told me that he no longer wanted to be married. So, after a couple of years we got a divorce and went our separate ways.

Now I'm a single mom with 2 kids and starting over! I went back to school and got my CNA license and started my career in nursing.

As a mom, you try to make sure your kids are well taken care of and then there are times you just need some help. I was homeless for about a month. My children slept on my friends couch. I didn't like it, but it's what I had to do.

I met this man whom I fell for and moved in with him. He went out with his friends and I stayed home with the kids. About 12:30 one Friday night, he came home drunk and talking crazy. He accused me of being out with another man and then jumped on me and beat me with his hands in my face, stomach and almost all over. I had to get out. I ran outside calling for help. Blood was running down my face and into my eyes, I couldn't see where I was going. I heard a voice asking, "Are you alright?"

As soon as I could close enough to see who it was I fell to the ground. It was one of my neighbors. I asked them if they could take me to the hospital and call my mother to come get my kids.

I went to the hospital. I ended up with 5 stitches over my right eye and had some bruises on my back and stomach. When my mom and family found out about what had happened to me, they wanted to kill him! But the law got him before they could. He served 5 years for assault on a female.

Now the hardest part about being a mom is not having the love of a mother. I can say this because she (my mom) gave me to her boyfriend (sexually) when I was 9 or 10 years old. How could she do this to me? I was her child. I still don't understand why my mom would let her boyfriend have sex with me. I ended up getting pregnant by this grown man when I was 12 years old and had to endure an abortion. Now what do you think they (the hospital staff) thought about me? I never wanted to be around people in the condition I was in. It felt like a horror story being unfolded at the seams.

But God had a plan for my life. I still don't know exactly what it is, but I'm still here and I help people as much as I can.

I am now happily married to the most wonderful man God could have sent me. He is warm, caring, affectionate and full of God's love. I couldn't have asked for anyone better! We have 8 beautiful children and 18 grandchildren. Sometimes I have to pinch myself to make sure I'm alive, and living in this most wonderful and precious time. When I read the Bible, it talks about how your children's children will be blessed of the Lord. At the time, I didn't see myself with grandchildren. But with six daughters, I should have known that I would live to see it.

God is so good to me, that's why I praise Him like I do!

A MOTHER'S AND GRANDMOTHER'S LOVE

Marilyn Bryant-Tucker

The Angels are watching over my Grandmother in heaven. My grandmother was my best friend. She loved me unconditionally. My grandmother held a special place for me in her heart. She took care of all her biological children, nieces, nephews, my sisters and I. She was a blanket of security to save us from all the problems we faced in our daily lives. She put us first. After my grandmother retired from her daily tasks, she would read the bible to us, tell us stories and different poems before sleeping at night.

Cooking was one of her favorite hobbies. She made sure we all ate well. I lived with my grandmother until the age of nine. I remember crying once telling my grandmother how I wished my skin was lighter because my mother and sisters were lighter. But she taught me to love my dark skin. She told me she wished her skin was as dark as my skin. She told me that she would sit in the sun for hours to get a suntan. Because of her encouraging words, I began to embrace my dark skin.

As a child, I had an entrepreneurial spirit. What a gift to possess, naturally! I remember as a child working in the garden with my grandmother. At the time, I did not realize how gifted and smart she was. I would sit in the garden, and watch her dig the dirt and put the seeds in to grow watermelons, collards, cabbages, potatoes,' cucumbers, squash, and so much more. At first and for quite some time there was no visible sign that anything was happening, and you could easily forget that something actually was. My grandmother would go into the garden often during the week and pull the weeds and water the garden and work to keep the pests out too. Then weeks later – I began to see the fruits and vegetables begin grow!

What I am saying? Growing a business is much like gardening.

I have learned few clichés from my grandmother such as:

- Do not put all your eggs in one basket.
- Never count your eggs before they hatch.

My grandmother helped prepare me for marriage and helped me understand the meaning of my wedding vows. I would watch how she loved my granddaddy during the time he had his health and strength and during the time he dealt with sickness from the stroke. My grandmother sat me down before I was married and explained to me, that there would be times when we could be mad and then in the very same hour love each other.

She loved family and gifted us with her love, and Southern cooking. She kept a clean home, made sure we went to church and sang in the church choir. The holidays were very special because of my grandmother. They were some of the best times. Our family would travel to my grandmother's home doing the holidays. I thank her for loving me unconditionally.

My mom is also a very sweet person who puts others before herself, she is amazing and she taught me to get an education and to be independent. She has many talents. She is a seamstress, fashion designer, caterer and floral designer. She developed a method of using turkey instead of pork for her barbecues and catering events. She didn't think people wouldn't like it 'because it had not yet been heard of, but now, it's become quite a staple for many. She helped create a BBQ sauce which became a big favorite at a local restaurant in my hometown.

I wish I had the knowledge about marketing then that I have today; because I could have helped her to become a successful business owner. I remember mom sewing my clothes while I was in middle school all the way through college. I would be nominated every year, through my dormitory, for being the best-dressed undergraduate at Fayetteville State University. My mom would see to it that my sisters, friends, classmates and I were well looked after.

I remember I started having sudden nose bleeds. My mom would not sleep until I felt better. My mother's love is the bond that connects us—the best moments in life are captured in memories. There are angels sent from God to guide us through our troubled times. I Thank God for my mother! She has been the rock through some of my storms. My mother motivates and encourages me. She is my mentor and role model.

She is Ms. Congeniality! My Mom has been honored as Home Town Hero by the Rocky Mount Elks Lodge. She is the Founder of Care and Give Volunteer Charity Foundation. She also started the charity foundation to encourage others to give an unselfish hand in order to help others, specifically to those who cannot help themselves and the elderly. She gives unselfishly and loves giving and helping others. She enjoys seeing other people smile.

A Mothers and grandmothers love help shape individuals and culture. As we see, there are many relationships in life. But one of the most powerful is that between the mother, grandmother and children. Every child needs this kind of support. Additionally, I am thankful to have had my grandmother's love and support. She left me with many glorious memories. My mother continues to carry on the support and love. To have a wonderful mother and grandmother is a glorious blessing.

MOTHER: BETTER KNOWN AS "MAMA HAZEL"

Joann Roberts

Mother, better known as "Mama Hazel" was a sacrificial Mother, an honorable wife, a strong phenomenal black woman who communicated love in all she did!

She was strict in her ways of teaching, but very loving in her approach. I remember when she was disciplining me, she'd do so with tears in her eyes at times.

Mother prepared us, as much as she could for the future. She taught us the necessities of cooking, house, yard, and personal hygiene. And how to behave in a respectful manner. Yes, good manners were highly demanded by our Mother! Oh, we did some stuff behind her back, but if she caught us, our rumps felt it for days!

Another great value our Mother taught and demanded of her children was church attendance! We had no car in my day, so we had to walk to Sunday school and church; sometimes three to five miles one way! Of course, it was a little safer then than now! When Evangelist Oral Roberts would come on the radio, Mother had us to lay our hands on the radio as means of contact when he was praying for the sick.

As I think about it now, The Lord has given to some the gift of healing and laying on of hands, along with other diverse gifts!

Another great value Mother taught her children was how to avoid trouble as much as you can: For instance, keep your hands out of your pockets or purse when shopping until you get to the register to check out! I still practice that today, especially with the cell phone ringing. She informed us that because we are black, people will watch us closer than others, and accuse us of stealing.

Some of her favorite sayings were: you going to reap what you sow; you don't miss your water 'til your well runs dry; every good-bye ain't gone, every shut eye ain't sleep; the longer you stir in mess, the longer it will stink... leave it alone, it'll dry up and the wind will blow away!

Mother was indeed a loving and wonderful Mother, grand-mother, great- great- great-grandmother!

WHAT MY MOTHER TAUGHT ME

Antonio McCarver

When most fifteen year olds are focusing on their sophomore year of high school, my fifteen-year-old mother and fourteen-year-old father were having to make plans on what to do with a baby boy that was on the way. Born to teenage parents in a time when you're ostracized for such abdominal acts, I learned strength, perseverance, and love from my mother.

Most parents can tell you that it's not easy to raise children; financially, emotionally, and spiritually, to be happy, healthy, and productive young men and women. Being a single father myself of two young ladies, I have had to rely on a level of strength that I have never known before; and I am a United States Marine. I have had to create money out of thin air, food from bare cupboards, and clothing and other resources on sheer prayer, faith, and resilience alone. It is during those times of, "God, how in the hell am I supposed to do this?" that I remember looking in the dictionary for the word strength and seeing my mother's picture.

Yes, the technical definition of strength, per the dictionary, is "mental power, force, or vigor", but my definition is "unyielding, unrelenting, and bending without breaking" and that definition came from watching my mother and my grandmother. I remember the times that my mother had to work multiple jobs, attend an alternative high school, and forgo enjoying the part of her life that we call "personal time", and do it all before ever graduating high school. My father, Thomas, being fifteen by the time that I was born, had to rely on what he knew in order to help my mother take care of me, and that was a life in the streets. Of course, taking care of a baby in the late 1970's, was a group and community effort. As my mother, Mechelle, and I grew together she knew that the street life that my father was living was a sure ticket to no-where fast, as well as, a life that she didn't want for their son.

While my father would resort to crack and cocaine as a source of income, my mother resorted to working multiple straight and narrow jobs. All the while making sure that every day there was a home-cooked meal for me to eat and a pleasant lunch in a brown paper bag for me to have whether at day care or school. As I have grown into a man, being married once upon a time in my life, to now being a full time single father, I have had to rely on those lessons from yesteryear to help me and my babies survive the trials of today. During a very tumultuous time of my life over the past couple of years, I asked my mother, "Ma, how can I do this? I don't know what to do?" It was her answer that provided me with the insight that I needed.

She said, "Son, you survive. That's how you do it! You pray and give it to God, then you listen, and then you go do what I taught you and you survive! You can do this son!"

If I'm being completely transparent and honest, this was not what I *"wanted"* to hear, but it was exactly what I needed to hear. I have seen my mother pawn her wedding ring to ensure that we have a meal to eat for Thanksgiving. Now any woman that has ever been married and in love will tell you that not having their wedding ring is one of the most hurtful, and gut-wrenching things that could happen to them. To see the emotional pain in her eyes as she rubbed her ring finger while attempting to smile and prepare a meal made of love, taught me a couple of things. The most important being that my mother is the true definition of Super Woman. I never heard her complain, but I did hear her in her prayer closet crying out to God for the "*Supernatural*" help. When adversity comes, we have to remember that, "those of us that never give up, never give in, and continue to fight, will win, as long as we don't give up" or in Biblical terms according to Galatians 6:9 "*Let us not become weary in doing good, for at the proper time we will reap a harvest if we do not give up*".

We can all turn to 1 Corinthians 13 and get a good sound definition of what love is and supposed to be, and yes, I try to live by those principles, but I first learned what love is from my mother. She taught me that love is not just a word but that it is compassion. It is sacrifice. Love is forgiving and kind. But most of all, love is a series of actions that reaches beyond who you are, to show what you are. It is love that allowed my mother to endure the hurt and pain of losing friends because she was the pregnant girl at fifteen, as if being pregnant was somehow contagious. It was love that allowed moved her to tears as she had to tell her son that someone had murdered his father. And it was love that allowed her to continue to be kind to me, compassionate to me, and still love me after I hurt her with words and actions.

Having children of my own, I have now come to realize those same things and learn those same lessons. Hugging my girls and telling them that everything is going to be alright when they've been hurt by someone that they love and trust, and feeling their pain deep down inside of my own heart, reminds me of that fateful night on June 13, 1987 when she(my mother) had to tell me that my hero was no longer alive. Or the times that my girls have reacted to life in ways that have caused them to say things that I am sure that they didn't mean, causing me to feel defeated, wounded, and inadequate, while still being willing to die for them is a testament to the love and forgiveness that I learned from my mother.

My mother taught me to honor and respect women. This might be why I am considered to be as charming as I am. But it is those lessons that have empowered me and equipped me to be able to raise daughters on my own. I can show them the love and compassion that mothers inherently have while also displaying the strength and protection that we tend to look for in our fathers. Mechelle Renee Glenn has been able to teach me how to be the best of both worlds without compromising the true essence of who God created me to be. The true inspiration behind Raleigh's first "Mother and Son Dance and Cancer Benefit" which I happened to have put together, came from the love that my mother has graced me with.

No matter the obstacle or the challenge in life, I have learned that there is virtue in the perseverance. At fifty-five years of age, my mother graduated from college with her Bachelor's degree and is on track to graduate over the next year with her Master's degree. It was this display of intestinal fortitude and diligence that encouraged me to enroll back in college at North Carolina A&T State University to complete the process that I started many years ago and obtain my Bachelor's degree. If my mother can persevere and endure the challenge at fifty-five years old, surely, I can do it at forty. In addition to, I have young ladies in college and preparing for college that I can now be an inspiration to and show that with persistence and dedication, we can accomplish any and every goal, dream, and ambition that our Heavenly Father has put into our heart. My mother showed me what it means to live out the scripture in Isaiah 40:31 *"But they that wait upon the Lord shall renew their strength; they shall mount up with wings as eagles; they shall run, and not be weary; and they shall walk, and not faint."*

To me, there is no greater display of perseverance than seeing a girl have a baby, grow into a young lady, grow into a woman and face discrimination, divorce, and homelessness while being a single mother and yet raise a boy into a man, all while doing it with love, grace, and dignity. My mother taught me what it means to love and forgive, strength when 're too weak to even give up, and perseverance when everything and everyone around you begins to fail and fall by the wayside. My mother taught me what it means to be a Super Hero. She's my Super Hero and now I have grown to be one for my babies.

A DIFFERENT KIND OF MOTHER'S LOVE

Alexis J. Green

My mother and I have a strange relationship. We talk but to me it strange. I think of a mother as one of those women who kiss your boo boo's, cooks all day, every day and plays dress up with her girls, etc. She isn't like that. She cooks, she cleans, she's very sassy but she just wasn't "that" type of mother.

Being that I was her first child, we had a strong bond in the beginning from what I am told, but then again, she never got up with me at night as a newborn and she wasn't great at doing hair either or had much patience. However, at a young age, I wanted to be around her all the time.

Fast forward five years and my sister is born. I took on the role of being her mother. My mother never neglected us but she just wasn't adorning or sweet or overly loving. She was about teaching us lessons, education and how to be successful in our careers, about finances and work ethic.

I saw my mother go to work EVERYDAY, never really taking vacation or sick time. She retired from the State of NC after 28 years of service. She has impeccable credit, a very nice nest egg, buys WHATEVER she wants and she is a great saver. She saved, she budgeted and very calculated in the way she spent and invested her money. She believed in taking care of things and not being wasteful.

When I turned 16, I wanted to get my driver's license. She didn't agree but went along with my dad. The stipulation was I would be responsible for my portion of the increase of the car insurance. It was then I was convinced my mother hated me. She always seemed to be so hard on me, never letting me take the easy road, never letting me slack off or even think about giving up. We didn't go prom dress shopping, we didn't get our nails or hair done together or anything most teenage girls and mother's do. At that time, she was the church secretary for a small church in her home town. What she taught me to do was be responsible and accountable and how to deal with money.

When I became a young mother at the age of 19, she was disappointed. To me, it was partially her fault. She never talked to me about sex or anything in relation to a boy. Nothing... ever... So I said, "You didn't tell me... how was I supposed to know?"

I had my son, came home from the hospital and the next day she went to work, like normal, didn't take any time off to see if I needed help, wanted help or even knew what to do. She didn't change anything about what she was doing.

As the years went on, I got older and made mistakes with my money, credit and finances. Not too many times did I have to ask her for help but when I did, she would help, but not without having to hear her mouth. That was one of the reason why I made sure I didn't have to ask her for much.

Age 26, I had my second son. She was quiet, didn't say much but she did tell me, You like to make things hard for yourself, don't you? I didn't understand the question at the time, but now I do.

Over the past 35 years, she has been teaching me the entire time. She hasn't taken pity on me or allowed me to use excuses, she has been teaching me lessons. Some I didn't realize until late in life. She is the reason I have been in the same field for the past 16 years. She is the reason, I am very funny about my money and how I hate to struggle financially. She is the reason why I push myself to be successful, even if I fail, I never give up. I have 7 friends and we are all the same age and they always tell me how much more mature I am then they are when it comes to finances. By no means, am I perfect. There is always room for improvement but I look back and often think... What was she really saying to me all those days when I would turn a deaf ear to her? When I would refuse to listen?

I asked her one day, "Why are you so hard on me and not my sister?"

She told me, ever since you were a baby and even when you begin to talk, some of your first words were, I can do it by myself. She said, you never needed me. You have always been independent, I knew as a little girl you were strong and you would be fine.

Now that I am a mother, I know her feelings. You want your kids to be better than you were. Not struggle, succeed by leaps and bounds and go farther than you can ever go. Sometimes, you have to make them uncomfortable and not let them have their way to prepare them for this worldly war. I want so much more for my sons than I had, have and will have.

When she asked me, you like making things hard for yourself don't you? I said, she is just being her typical self, but she was right. Being a parent is a privilege not to be taken lightly. God trusts us with his perfect gifts and we are supposed to do right by them. As humans, we are selfish so we do what we want. Being a parent is the most selfless act of all. Looking through the eyes of a mother, I realize all she wanted me to do is be able to take care of them, provide for them and give them the life they deserved.

That's my motivation for all I do. To give, be and provide the best for them. So now that I'm older, I realize, it wasn't that she didn't love me. She was teaching me, showing me and providing an example for me to be better. She was preparing me to be better. She was challenging me to be great!

Love comes in many ways, forms and actions.

She showed hers the best way she knew how, a different kind of love.

MEMORIES OF MOM

April Dozier

Being that my mom passed when I was 19, I felt slighted by God. I felt like I had to learn life fast. No more asking my Mom questions about life. No more of mom coming up to me with her discerning spirit asking me what's wrong and making me express my feelings.

As time went on, I began to heal.

I am now 35 years old, married, and raising a super energetic four-year-old. I've been missing her (my mom) now more than ever because I'm evolving. I often tell God that if I didn't need her then, I definitely need her now.

Normally, Mothers spend most of their lives raising their daughters, and then becoming friends with them when they are adults. So now it's like okay God, I want my friend, but God with His loving and amazing self has surrounded me with so many women who pour into me.

Now I have my four-year-old and I catch myself doing the exact things my mom used to do. Like how I stand when talking stern to my daughter, and how much I love God like she did. Oh, and I can't forget how much she loved to dance, and I love dancing as well. So, I can say that I'm forever learning from my mom because she lives in me. I have her characteristics and she's forever teaching me something.

At the early age of five, I remember watching my Mom applying her makeup and doing her hair. She was always one for beauty. Whatever makeup she stopped using, she let me play in! Playing makeup was so fun! She had so much makeup. Mom shared with me that she used to be a beauty consultant and actually did make-up for people on the side. A makeup artist wasn't as popular back then as it is now, so she stopped pursuing it and continued her work in other areas.

My Mom also loved helping people. It was nothing for her to visit someone and helping them with whatever they needed. Whether it was bringing food to someone who's been sick or just sitting and keeping them company. As I look back at all of those wonderful things, I am realizing that my Mom left a legacy for my family to continue to build. All four of my siblings has a piece of my Mom in them. My brothers are so humorous, always making someone smile and such hard workers. I know they got that from my Mom and Dad. My sister loves people, and she loves to visit people to make sure they are okay just like Mom did. I inherited the love of makeup from Mom. I am now a licensed esthetician and makeup artist. Even her oldest grand-child inherited the love of fashion and clothing like her grandmother!

She was all of these things and more! From a lover of fashion/beauty, dancing, laughing, to helping others and family. I truly believe God makes no mistakes when He called her home. Sometimes God has to remove your crutch in order to tap into what He has placed inside of you.

We relied so much on my Mom. It's been 16 years since she's passed away and it feels like it all happened yesterday. Some years, I'm great and the memories fade. Then I may have a season where I think about her almost every day. Sometimes, I look at her jewelry and her work badge from Belk's in Crabtree. I begin thinking about the times when I would call her at work to talk about nothing!

I think I coped better before marriage than after marriage. I say this because when I was single, I stayed occupied, and I was young. I am now married and have been married for 12 years. We have a beautiful daughter who looks just like Mom with such an energetic personality. I'm evolving, and forever changing. Oh, how I long to hear her voice and receive her wisdom. Every day is a learning experience, and all I can do is take life one day at a time. I cherish my family with all of my heart because I know that life is not promised to us. My mom was here one day and gone the next.

I have such a tender heart for mothers and daughters. It bothers me when a mother and daughter do not get along. It's easy to forgive, mend, and let the healing process begin. Sometimes we make forgiveness so hard for ourselves. It also warms my heart to see mothers and daughters who have a tight bond. My daughter and I are very close—not only is she my only child, but she's my miracle child.

My husband and I had been trying to conceive a child for almost seven years. We couldn't figure out for the life of us, why we couldn't get pregnant. I definitely felt slighted by God around that time.

Here I am, Motherless, and childless. I'm like okay God, are you punishing me for something I've done? I felt hurt, abandoned, guilty, depressed, less than woman, angry, and all of the above! My husband was my greatest support during that time because he desired a child as well.

———

In year of 2011, we went to a conception specialist to nail down the issue. Come to find out, I had PCOS (polycystic ovarian syndrome). The doctors said this was the cause of my infertility.

After we got the news, my husband and I decided to just give it all the God and rest in Him. During that same year, on Christmas Eve I took a test and it was positive! I cried like a baby! I thought God had forgotten about me! He didn't and he never did. Not only did He allow us to have a baby, but gave me a little girl, because God knew what I needed. He knew that I desired to have a beautiful bond with my daughter just like I had with my mom.

My advice to Mothers out there, love on your daughters and nurture them. Pour out your wisdom every day. Be transparent at a time when they can handle it. Let your daughters know that it's okay to express their feelings and share their hearts. Daughters, take care of your Mothers. Listen to them and take their advice. Honor them with your words and gifts. Spend time with them and call them often. I sit and watch her play in my makeup. It reminds me of just how I would play in my Mom's makeup. I love and cherish my bond with my daughter.

Thank you, Mom for being in my heart.

THE LEGACY OF A ROSE

Tajala Lockhart

My mother ran her life, like a one woman show. She had goals and ambitions. She pushed through many obstacles because she was determined to win. My mother was very inspired by a flower called the Rose, so much that she named her businesses after it "Thee Rose Hair Studio." Early in life, I had no idea why the Rose was such an inspiration to her.

However, day in and day out, I saw my mother work in the hospitality industry and then enter an industry where she eventually dominated for 25+ years. I had an opportunity as young girl to have a front row seat to watch her build from the ground up. It's hard to explain, but she didn't go about life teaching me lessons. However, I believe that she truly hoped that I was watching. She didn't have that from her mother, so it was hard for her to teach when she had not been taught.

The one thing that she made sure that she taught me was about God and faith. She knew from the Bible that a parent was responsible for his or her child biblically and spiritually until they turned 18 years of age. I believe that though, I was a very quiet young lady and didn't always understanding why at the time she was such a hard worker and believer. I learned so much from her and I see a lot of her in myself now at times that I am older.

I lost my beloved Rose in 2012. It wasn't until then that I connected to my mother in a way that was indescribable. My relationship with my mother now is such a special one. I have since learn that the Rose is symbolic of God at work in whatever situation they appear. That's who she was and what she delivered in the salon to her clients. Sometimes people didn't understand her uniqueness, her need to be stern and firm, however, she lived her life like a Rose.

She made sure that her insides were nurtured with God's word and her outside, her body, was taken care of through her talents which represent the petals of a Rose. However, her sternness and firmness are the thorns that she used to protect herself from all things negative.

I learned she was a journal writer, however it was not what most do in a journal. We write about our daily life and possible struggles and such. My mother journaled about her clients, co-workers, friends, myself, my husband, and my daughter. Her journals were selfless prayers. They were prayers for what they were going through and speaking life into things that wanted to do and asking God to open doors. Until this day, I don't know some of the people, but I am grateful to know that she everything that I would and could ever have in a mother. She was a Rose in every sense of the meaning.

What I have learned from her over the years, is that you have be the Rose that you want to be. However, you don't have to do it alone. She did everything by herself and I am doing the same thing. If you can't find the right people with the same passion— do it on your own.

I run my own businesses with two different partners and I have learned how to better manage my finances by watching a successfully Master Hairstylist run hers by walking around with all her earnings in her purse or in the home. My mother owned businesses that were both successful and unsuccessful in North Carolina and Georgia—she gave me a front seat to how to run a salon years ago, but I didn't understand the lessons until now.

The ultimate lesson is that pride got in the way and her health took over her life.

I now ensure that I find a healthy balance in trying to be successful, happy, healthy, and have a family--something she and I never had. It was just the two of us. A single rose trying to raise her rose bud with the best tools and teachings that she knew. I now am a Rose raising a rose bud with some of the tools that my mother used and with some new ones that I learned from others.

I am an only child in every sense of the words now. My life lesson is that my mother was the mother meant for me. She was the best mother in her flesh and the ultimate mother to me in spirit

As I reflect, I see my life mimicking hers in some ways. I am a Licensed Manicurist, currently have been in the Hospitality Industry for 28 years but, no, I am not journaling. However, I am teaching Hospitality to at risk youth and pouring into other lives. All the work that my mother tried to ensure that I learned about faith and on a spiritual level will never go away. It's in my blood. I will forever continue to be the best Rose I can be, so I can leave the Legacy of a Rose behind for my daughter.

RUTH MAE JACKSON DUNN

Debra Robertson

September 30, 1932-February 6, 2014

Ma, Mama, Mother, Mom, Mommy, Grandma, and Nana were some of the titles given to Mom... the epitome of a *"Virtuous Woman";* none other, like our mother.

"Ma," as I called her, grew up on a farm where she was taught the principles of hard work and survival. She taught us those same principles. She was the youngest and the daintiness of two girls reared under the candid instructions of a mother much like herself. She was deeply loved by her only sibling, her sister. Her father died when she was just two, but her grandfather stepped up to the plate to help his daughter rear the two.

Every day, especially school days, "Ma" would rise before the chickens, fully dressed to enter the kitchen. We would hear her hum one of her favorite spirituals as she took her time to make those mouth-watering homemade biscuits. *"Get up, make your bed, wash up, dress, and comb your hair, breakfast is almost ready, no time to spare!"* As we sat down to eat while she made sure daddy was up and not sound asleep, she would yell across the way, "Don't forget to say your blessing." This was one of her spiritual lessons.

Mama was graceful, poised and knew how to dress; often making her own and our clothes. A "hat diva," many shapes, colors and sizes often adorned her crown. Matching shoes and purses were her added delight and definitely stockings, not torn. A psalmist, lover of music, especially Gospel and quartet, always in church, never a stranger she met.

She was a fantastic cook, a wonderful baker, our strength when we were weak. She was the counselor who withstood many storms and possessed a love that always kept us nestled and warm. She was a provider of little, yet creator of much; a nurse when we got sick, indeed unrehearsed.

Mommy was not only a dedicated mother, but our banker too! Financial woes were often cared for from the white handkerchief or behind her closed bedroom door. The apple of our father's eye, the first he taught how to tie his tie.

Nana, grandma as the grandchildren would ask, "What did you cook today?"

"Whatever, you are welcome but if you don't eat it all do me a favor and save it for later. I left your cup with the rest with each of your names on one of them, so no need to ask for another, claim yours and not your sister's or brother's."

She helped many in need, never resisting the opportunity to feed. A Mother, a lady, a counselor, a nurse, a dedicated wife, a social diva, she could also be. She loved life and the joy of laughter. When things didn't go right, one would know; she'll repeat her favorite line you see – *"Woo Wee"*.

So "Mama," we thank you for the spiritual lessons and the work ethics you taught. Our hair is done, our slip is up, stockings not torn, our tie straight, our shirt tucked in, our bed made and our blessings said!

Ma, on behalf of all of us, I give you honor for the fruit of her hands. We praise your works!

MY MOM: DOROTHY J. DEBNAM

Gloria V. Debnam

When you meet my mother, the first things you notice are her bright smile and quiet demeanor. But what is behind the smile? My mother recently celebrated her 75th birthday. Knowing that mom is not one for a lot of fan fair, I arranged to have a few family members join us for brunch at a restaurant in downtown Raleigh. The mood was festive and enjoyed by all as we celebrated our mother, grandmother, sister-in-law, and aunt. For the days following the celebration, my mother received several calls and cards in recognition of her milestone birthday. With child-like appreciation, my mom expressed delight in the thoughtfulness of others. She seemed surprised that people thought so much of her and took the time to let her know. As I ponder it all, I realize how my mother has been an "unsung hero" in our family. What she did out of love came to be what we expected.

Raised in a large family (five girls and five boys), my mother learned early about sharing and going without many of the things my generation take for granted. Things like new clothes, full-course meals, the opportunity to go to college, having a career, and the chance to live on your own prior to getting married and raising a family. My mother married my father and traveled with him during his military career until he retired and moved back to his hometown of Raleigh, NC. Over the course of his 30+ year career in the Air Force, my parents had six daughters. My two youngest sisters were born after we relocated to Raleigh.

As a homemaker, my mom tirelessly maintained our home while my dad worked. Not an easy task. Despite all the meals prepared, laundry cleaned, and hair combed, my mom always, always, always had a "hymn in her heart." In fact, we often heard her singing as she worked throughout the day. I can only imagine what may have been going through her mind as she sang. Perhaps recalling the lyrics of church hymns helped her maintain her sanity amidst all the chaos eight girls can bring.

Fast forward past my sisters and I growing up... past my mother meeting my older brother Kirk and welcoming him as part of our family... past her working part-time as a house keeper... past caring for grandchildren during their early years and past taking care of my dad as his health declined. Over the years, my mother sacrificed endlessly so that her husband, children, and grandchildren were taken care of. Never one to complain or demand her way, there is no way that we can give her what she deserves. It's easy to give her gifts on her birthday, Mother's Day, and at Christmas. However, we have to be intentional about not taking her for granted in these later years of her life.

We must "give her flowers while she can smell them." Flowers to her include: a meal at K&W, going to a movie, walking around the track at Chavis Park, thanking her for a meal she's prepared, helping with household chores, gladly taking her to doctor appointments, or sitting outside on the bench in the backyard to soak up vitamin D.

The following verses from Proverbs 31 describe my mother Dorothy J. Debnam:

> "26 She speaks with wisdom, and faithful instruction is on her tongue.

27 *She watches over the affairs of her household and does not eat the bread of idleness.*

28 *Her children arise and call her blessed; her husband also, and he praises her:*

29 *"Many women do noble things, but you surpass them all."*

30 *Charm is deceptive, and beauty is fleeting; but a woman who fears the LORD is to be praised.*

31 *Honor her for all that her hands have done, and let her works bring her praise at the city gate."*

LETTER TO MY MOTHER: CAROLYN DAVIS GREEN

Michelle Green-King

I want to thank you, Mom, for living such a gracious life. You were such a prestigious Lady, I watched your elegance and was just always in awe of your regal resemblance fit for a monarch and especially your magnificent and dignified personality. So beautiful, you spoke to me always using your perfect grammar but still so kind. The way you blinked your eyes when you looked at me I knew every time you closed them it meant I Love you. You would stare at me to gain my attention so I could feel the transfer of love without you saying one word even in your time of transcending. The passion you showed in everything you did for me was so perfect. You told me I was your darling and such a beautiful girl. You said it every day. You had such high self-esteem that it automatically transferred to me. It was an expectation. You believed in education and you were such an educated lady yourself. Your legacy is superior, refined, beauteous, and statuesque. You always said folks will knock you down, but they can't take away your education and where you come from. Even in your struggle you will always have those two things.

Known to all, you were affectionately called "Foxy Brown!" You were the best dressed Lady they say in all of Raleigh. I've never seen you leave home without your makeup or undergarments. My Children and I have watch you put what looked like body armor on before started your day. Shaped like a Coke Cola bottle with nothing out of place in every garment you wore. Jewelry, matching purse, and gloves. You sure knew how to bring it! I still can't keep up but manage to do all those things only on special occasions. I'm still trying to figure out how you even felt like it every day. Not to mention, the wigs all around the room named after Famous people, Mary J, Halle Berry, Naomi Sims, to name a few. My children and I have watched you countless times Slay. Then comes the "Sun shades" as you called them. There was a pair to match every outfit, kept in the side of your car door and glove box. I remember we would have to wait while you fumbled through them to fine the perfect ones. You would turn on your Sam Cooke or O'Jays CD's and then the ride thru town would begin, never on the belt line. Only Nigel had the nerve to touch your radio, and you would chastise him every time. Oh, how I remember those days.

You always treated by me and my children with so much love. Constantly showering us with gifts and money. We all knew you had a favorite though. That Alton, was your Pride and Joy. Then came Greenleigh, who you use to somehow dress her just like you down to the faux furs.

I remember you used to tell me when I had Cryslyn I had one for myself since I had to share the children with Grand Parents. I just remember you were the busiest even after you retired from Wake County Schools. Seems 33 years of teaching wasn't enough, so you taught Adult Education at Wake Technical College and recruited kids to college at Shaw University. You were always at the Church where you served as Head Warden or attending an Association meeting and playing Bridge with your friends. You once told me if you stop working or being busy you will die. Once your service was up and your body wasn't physically able to drive you still wanted to inspire others. I made you stay home and take it easy. I remember teasing you because I could see things changing and your sharpness in your mind was different. I would say Mom, what is 2+2 and you would look at me with a frustrated face and say, "4 child."

We would laugh together as I said, "Girl you getting a little slow."

Yet, we didn't know that what you said was happening right before my eyes... you were going to leave me.

We are always reminiscing about all of the fond memories of you. I don't really have any bad ones because you always stood by our sides and made it better. You would get us straight in such a shrewd way and the words cut deep enough that we knew how much you loved us because of what you were willing to sacrifice and always put it all on the line for us.

You wrote a letter to me on my 40th birthday that I treasure and remember it as if you were reciting poetry to me. It read:

My dearest Michele on this day your 40th birthday, I am wishing you all the happiness there is to give. I want to thank you for being a thoughtful and wonderful daughter."

It continues, *"You must know how much I appreciate all the care you gave me while I was ill being sure that I had proper medical care and the endless hours you took care of me...You are one Special Girl! I will always think of the beautiful smile you show when you are happy. The understanding you show others. I am happy to see this day and share this day with you.*

My mother then shared the most important advice I may not have understood then, but now I experience it every day. *Always love your beautiful daughters just as I have loved you, give them your best and they will always be with you. Love your sons as they are only trying to find their way in the world. They will always come home to you*

The last thing she wrote is: *Age brings on change, and remember I Love you very much.*

Every time I read this letter I cry like a hurt child. I miss you so much. I've never loved someone so much. You were always my biggest cheerleader and you bragged about me to everyone. Even after you've left me, I hear from everyone that you loved me something crazy.

Mom, you were amazing and I try every day to just be half of what you were—this seems to sometimes be all I'm capable of. I just love you and when I lost you, I've never been able to find that type of love again. I will always cherish every memory of you.

My heart remains broken, but I manage to mend it together with the love you have left me. It sometimes feels like hanging shreds of a piece of distressed material. I manage to somehow keep going with what's left though. The thoughts of you give me Joy and I think of you each and every day. You're simply just unforgettable.

Love,
Darling Michele

WAITING THROUGH THE DARK CLOUDS

Karen Jones

Everyone has heard the stories of living in the South, going to Gramm's to spend the summer breaks... you learned so much from Gramm's wisdom and her grace... My mom learned from her mother the importance of caring, listening, learning and loving herself and God. God has always been the center of our family values giving us the faith, belief and power to endure good and bad times.

My mom worked hard to raise us the way God intended. She knew her daughters needed to see her push through hard times, challenges and some storms, yet trust her word and know, "God is always there. "

Mom showed us in many ways that going through storms didn't kill a person, but made them stop and wait to hear from God.

"Not to rush and go your own way but to be still and know God," she said, "You don't disrespect or disregard Gods power." So, the question is: when going through storms in life, how should I respond?

Well, I grew up in a home of reverence to God. We had one hard rule they we all had issues with because stopping our kickball games, our hopscotch or baseball games was not in our plans. A thunderstorm would arise, changing our whole play time. We had to stop what we were doing, no matter what and sit still. This means no TV, no talking, no playing "God is working"... So as children we knew the drill... no matter where we were! It was a good way to keep all of us quiet and eventually it turned into a nap!

With the loud claps of thunder, rain and wind, we would sit in the front room, in the dark and waiting for the storms to pass over. We knew that the storm would end and the sun would shine once more. We would be alright. God wasn't angry, He was just working. It has taught us that in our own lives that storms will come but soon the clouds and bright lights, and the big claps of thunder wouldn't stay always. All we had to know was that we were to reverence God and relax.

What a powerful lesson of waiting through the dark clouds.

One afternoon while watching a movie on our basement floor... a storm began to rise in the middle of our movie! We were so into this movie, we forgot the rules!

My mom yelled "turn that TV off; it's stormy!"

With great disappointment, and dismay, we reluctantly turned it off. We looked at each other and said, "We gonna' miss the end."

We waited in the quietness for as long as we could. We thought the storm had passed over or we wanted the storm to be gone, so we did the unthinkable. We couldn't miss the end of that movie; it was so good! Back in the day, there was no rewind, on demand, rentals or a way record it. We were gonna' miss it! Reluctantly, we decided to turn the TV back on. We kept the volume down, so mom wouldn't hear it and started to watch that good movie (don't even remember the name). After all, we were taught to reverence God and that this storm was a time of reflection, a time to be still, a time to let God do His work.

We worried about a movie... Lol!

That big floor model TV played for maybe five to seven minutes and the loudest crackle pop, the biggest roar and claps of thunder came out of nowhere... Our eyes grew big as cantaloupes because we realized that the storm had not passed.

We had done it! In a matter of seconds came the biggest lightning bolt! I literally saw a bright light and loud pop like a mini bomb hit the antenna on the house! It hit the TV. It narrowly missed me and blackened the floor just in front of me.

I jumped, screaming and running up the stairs terrifying my mom.

"Mom... Mom!"

She came running. "What is it? What happened? What was that?"

The TV had popped, making the loudest noise with smoke coming from it and from the tan tile I had been sitting on.

I'm yelling that the lightning hit inside the house and hit the TV and almost hit me.

She said, "I told you to cut that TV off."

We had broken the rules and turned it back on, we had not "waited through the dark clouds," and we tried to rush God and His work. We were punished without mom touching us. We learned a great lesson. Wait through the storms and don't rush God. No earthly pleasure is worth disobeying God or your mom.

There *are* consequences to your actions. It's not always about what you want to do—it's not about your timing, and it's about waiting through the process. Let God speak while you listen.

Wait and wait.

Know that God knows and sees what's going on and there are reasons why you must wait. Rest and take a nap through the storm! Just wait through those dark clouds.

WHAT DID I LEARN FROM MY MOTHER?

Arlinda Rodriguez

My mother was a small woman with a big voice who loved to have fun with her friends. What I learned from her was that I must always be able provide and take care of myself and not depend on a man to do so. Her advice has served well and not so well at times. But it has made me strong and unafraid to pursue dreams and goals that will sustain me. She was an honest woman who would tell you what you needed to hear, even when you didn't ask. She always encouraged me to pursue my dreams and stand on my own. She always reminded me that God is always in control and to trust in him. She was the queen of making up words and figures of speech that made you laugh. My mother was a hard worker who worked for the same company for 40 plus years. Though we went without some of the things we wanted as a child, mother made sure we had all that we needed.

My mother was not a nurturing person and in some senses, I believe we grew up together. She had me in her early twenties and never had a true opportunity to experience life. I used to think back over my life and feel sad that I didn't have a traditional mother, someone who you did girly thing with--someone who gave you advice on womanhood and life, or was a shoulder to cry on when you were down. Sometimes on a school night, my mother would have a party with all her friends over. We would tell her we couldn't sleep because of the loud music and she would tell us "if you're sleepy, you got to sleep."

I laugh about that now, but it was not funny back then. One day I decided that I would not dwell on the things my mother did not teach me and focus on the advice she gave me, accepting the fact that my mother was who she was. Once I acknowledged that, I developed a closer relationship with her.

I knew my mother was proud of me, but I don't remember telling me so. I used to get frustrated with her because I used to see how she always did everything for my sister and her children. She made sure they had everything they needed, but she never asked what I needed or if my daughter needed anything. One day I got so frustrated about it that I confronted her. Her response was that she never asked me if I needed her support or help with anything because I have always been able to care of myself. That was when I realized that was her way of showing me how proud she was of me.

It was not until her transition that friends and family would tell me how much she bragged about the things I had accomplished, and how I have always made sure she had what she needed. I recognized that everyone loves and appreciates you in their own way.

I must admit that I took her advice of being strong and independent to such extents that I have lost relationships, but as I got older I learned to balance it all. One thing for sure is that my mother was always ride or die if I needed her. If she found out that someone had harmed me in any way, she was always ready to give them a good cursing out. This still make me laugh today.

My mother transitioned from life to eternity in November of 2016, and her presence is so greatly missed. I still have difficulty accepting she is not here. I find peace in knowing that I was there to care for her during her short period of illness until the end. I made sure she knew she was loved and ensured that she rededicated her life to Christ the day before she transitioned.

When I think about it, what I went through pushed me to be more loving and more open; I also understand how to be a support to my friends and I am not afraid to step out on my own.

My advice to others is to appreciate the mother that you have. Accept and love them for who they are. No one was born with all the answers and there are no rules to motherhood. I realized my mother loved me more than I could understand because I was too focused on her being a June Cleaver.

MY MOTHER, MY FRIEND, MY MENTOR

Beth Wright-Jefferson

I rarely asked my mother how to do anything because I was more of an observer. However, what I observed over the years is phenomenal. I always wondered how my mother kept up with everything in the house; the bills, groceries, my school shenanigans, clothes and everything else. So again, I watched her. She used to open the mail, write a note and make stacks on her desk. She made shopping for groceries look like an art form. She was very strategic in her approach, crossing items off her list as she strolled down every isle. I was always in awe that she knew exactly how much her groceries would cost before she got to the register. She knew if an item was priced incorrectly or not.

She entered the kitchen with grace and created a meal made for a king every evening. Without asking, I continued to just watch her. She ruled the house, often without raising her voice, sternly and without fail. She delegated chores amongst my siblings and we dare not challenge her. In all of this, I learned how to run my own home.

As I reached adulthood and set up my own house, I found that I learned more from my mother than even I realized. As my bills began to come in, I set them aside by category. I later opened each one, writing the balance due and due date on the outside of the envelope. I restacked them—not only by category, but by my payday. When I think about what my mother did and how I continue to do today, I smile internally. I smile mainly because without a word, my mother taught me how to keep my bills paid in full and on time. When my money didn't stretch as far as my bills, I referenced my note on the outside of the envelope and adjusted my plan for payment. So, this is how she kept everything running in the house. Everything she did with the bills make sense now that I am an adult. Although nothing fancy occurred, she taught me to how to be a good steward over my bills and my finances.

As I enter the grocery store, I am armed with my grocery list, whether mentally or written down. I start on the far end of the store and work my way around, just as my mother did so many years before. Sometimes I pause at certain bargains and think briefly, "What would my mother do?" She stressed frequently to me how important it was to know the prices of the items you're buying to identify good deals. Often, I nodded, but not really being too concerned at what she was saying. Now I find myself mimicking her in the grocery store, even down to how I approach sales and buying in bulk.

I never realized that her approach in the grocery store had everything to do with her ability to have a well-balanced meal every evening. As I move through the grocery store, I think about what I have in my refrigerator, in my freezer, in my pantry and I do a quick menu in my head for the week. It hits me, this is how my mother did it! Without conversation and a lot of debate, she taught me how to maneuver in the grocery store and run my kitchen just as she did when I was growing up.

When I walk through my house and think about my child-hood, I laugh as if someone has just told me the joke of the century. Growing up, my mother used to say that she hated the day that I would have to keep house. Frankly, I was a daddy's girl. Although I watched my mother and how she ran the house, I was much more interested in following behind my father outside and it was obvious. Whenever my mother would tell me to do chores or anything in the house, I rushed through it without interest or care in doing it correctly. She would always choose me to be the one that would grow up with a messy house because of my lack of interest. Funny. In looking at my house and thinking of how I meticulously clean, organize and decorate, I think that it is the one thing that my mother got wrong. But I realized, it was her approach in running her house that instilled in me to keep my house put together and clean. She didn't stand for it and neither do I. So again, without a long message, my mother taught me a valuable lesson in housekeeping.

I gained an immense amount of knowledge from my mother, most of which she probably is not completely aware. She is a creature of habit but for some reason, growing up under her roof was never bored. She stayed home with me until I started first grade. I skipped kindergarten because as soon as I was able, she taught to read and write by giving me the newspaper as she read it. I never went without new clothes; for school, the summer, or winter, although I could have easily been made to wear handy downs from my older sisters. She made sure we went on vacation at least twice a year; spring break and summer vacation. I know she had the help and support of my father, but even he depended on her to be a great mother, friend and wife.

There are many things that my mother taught me, but I couldn't mention one without mentioning the majority of them. Paying bills, keeping the house running, grocery shopping, and maintaining your house... the list goes on. Her character while raising her children, especially me, was unwavering. Just from observing her; learning her actions and reactions to so many different obstacles over the years, she has taught me how to be a woman, a professional, a friend, a wife and so much more. So yes, when I think of my mother and my friend, she swiftly becomes my mentor.

With love and honor, she is my queen.

BRENDA

Marsha Perry

The truth is that I never really had a chance to know and enjoy my mother. I was five years in kindergarten when my mother passed away. What I was told is that she was a God-fearing, Educated, Resilient woman. There are so many things I wish I could have shared with my mom. As I got older, the memories faded and I grew angry. All my life, I longed for the mother I knew I would never physically see again.

Through the highest peaks and lowest valleys of my life I would always think of my mother. The best memories of my mother were when she took me to kindergarten. I remembered her standing at the door smiling for a very long time.

The grief that came with the early loss of my mother caused such a rhythmic movement through most of my life. There is absolutely nothing in life that can replace your mother. Most of my life I had a keen sense of isolation and a sharp awareness of my own mortality. When all else had failed or disappointed me in my life, I'd always wish that my mother was here to talk to me. I share a lot of similarities of my mother. She was also a teen mother who overcame obstacles to raise my older sister. My older sister often reminds me of the kindness that mother always showed towards others.

Brenda Faye Bass was born on January 11, 1955 from Raleigh NC. She was the youngest of eight children. My mother had her first child at sixteen years of age. She continued her education earning a diploma, later to also earn B.S. in Business from Hard Barger Junior College. It's funny while writing this I found out how much I did not know about my mother. I knew the basic information and I guess that was enough. My mother loved her family and her church. She was a dedicated member of First Church of God in Raleigh NC. A tremendous giver, she would extend help to any and all that needed her.

I remember talking to my grandmother before her passing, asking her things about my mother. She would always tear up before she started to talk. I felt guilty asking her because I did not want to make her cry. She always told me how much my mother loved me and my sisters. As an inquisitive individual, that just never sat well with me.

I remember going on a weekend trip with a close cousin. As we were having dinner one night, I asked her about my mother. She looked at me and I quickly said, "Yes, I know my mother love me, everyone tells me that. Give it to me. Tell me what no one else will say about my mother."

She looked me in my eyes and said, "Your mother was not happy in her marriage, Marsha and was about to divorce your father."

I asked, "Why?"

She stated, "Your father cheated on your mother consistently and was a constant verbal abuser."

This was a total shocker.

My hero, the man that could do no wrong in my eyes was no different from the jackass that I was married to once. That information that my cousin shared with me that weekend answered so many question in my life. I wondered why no one would tell me, but I guess it was to spare my feelings. After that weekend, I wondered if my mother ever tried to seek help. Did anyone know what was going on and just did nothing?

It wasn't until later in my life that I decided that I had to deal with the grief of my mother's passing. The feeling that I'd suppressed for such a long time had to go. Grief is like that; it intensifies every loss. I began to seek help. It aided me with my own personal journey of abuse and depression that I was dealing with at that time. I wanted to do things different for my mother sake.

I tell myself, "Marsha, you will be the bloom in your mother's tulip garden, flourishing in a healthy state of beauty and beauty. My mother's time here on earth was short-lived, but has left a great impact. I learned to adapt to a whole new way of living. She left great memories with many people. Her smile was the lemonade to her life-lived lemons.

THINGS I LEARNED FROM MY MOTHER: JOENELL SUMMERFIELD A.K.A "MAMA JOE OR PASTOR J"

Valisha Summerfield

There are so many things that I admire about my mother and many things I've learned from my mother over the years. Growing up I always wanted to be just like or just as good as my mom. I watched my mom cook, clean, wash clothes, work a job; take care of me and my siblings; sew and make clothes for me and my siblings; help with homework and so much more. There's really not enough I could say about how much my mom means to me. First of all, she is a TRUE woman of God, POWERFUL, full of Love, a great listener, STRONG, and a FIGHTER. Yep, she's my Superwoman who is so full of the Spirit and wisdom of God.

The Facts of Life:

I thank God that I've been so blessed with a mom that talked to me about things EVERY girl needs to learn from her mother. I remember when I was between the ages of 8 and 10 years old, my mom talked to me about menstruation and gave me reading material about the what, whys and how when it came to the different things that happen within a girl's body. My mom schooled me very well about what to expect and what to do should I get my period while at school, church, a relative/friend's house, etc. I like to say that timing is everything because little did my mom know, she was preparing me for what was about to happen real soon. While at the tender age of 10, I got my first period. I remember that day like it was yesterday. I was actually at home when it happened, but my mom was not there as she had just given birth to my younger brother at the time. I'm so thankful to this day that she talked to me about that way before it happened because I knew exactly what to do. She had previously shown me where to look in her bathroom cabinet for the necessary female products and she had also shown me what to do in a situation when there are no sanitary napkins to use.

I thank God EVERYDAY for the things she has taught me over the years. I've always told myself that when I have a daughter I want to be sure I do just as good of a job in raising her just as my mom raised and trained me. I want to instill a lot of the same great values and life principles that my mom instilled in me. She exemplifies a true virtuous woman of God just as Proverbs 31 talks about.

My Mom's Sound Advice on Relationships:

As I sit and think about the relationships that didn't work out I recall the times that I had just broken up with a guy and would feel so bad about the fact that I either wasted so much time dealing with that person. I would end up talking to my mom about how the relationship went sour and I remember certain statements she would make such as, *"Well Lisha, There's no need for you to beat yourself up about what happened...it didn't work out and it's okay. The key is to ask yourself, 'What did I learn from this or out of this that I wouldn't do again or how are you going to move forward after this?"* She taught me if you need to cry, cry for a little bit, but don't stay there. Pick yourself up, dust yourself off and *"KEEP IT MOVIN."*

That advice meant the world to me in what seem to be a difficult time in my life which was after a break-up with a guy. My mom taught me that there was no need to be all depressed over a guy. She would say things like, *"Lisha, you don't ever want to just lose your mind over some man. God should always come first in your life and seek God and let the Holy Spirit lead you when it comes to whether or not a young man is right for you."* Mom would tell me to watch for *"Red Flags"* in a relationship.

To this day, my mom will tell you that a woman always knows and to listen to the Holy Spirit. I appreciate how my mom never just jumped so quickly to judge someone that I was dating right off the bat. My mom is an observer so I knew she was watching from a far, but at the same time I always respected her wisdom and insight as a woman and mother. As an avid reader, my mom would always purchase great books whether it be inspirational, Christian living, or practical living. Somehow, she would always come across a book for me that she felt would be a good read for me. I never took that for granted because those particular books she would purchase for me would come at just the right time in my life, which made it even more special. My mom has always been big on allowing me and my siblings to make our own decisions whether it was who we were dating or just other life decisions in general. Her thing was that she never wanted to be a negative influence when it came to me or my siblings were dating.

Of course, my mom has always wanted me to make the right decision when it came to dating and marriage. However, she would say that ultimately the choice is ours and we're the ones that would be married to the person and have to live with the choices that we make. Her prayers for me and my siblings have always been that we let the Holy Spirit lead us and guide us when it came to making sound decisions on who to marry as well as other life decisions. I so love the GOD in my mom!

#mymomrocks.

When Life Knocks You Down:

Amongst the many life challenges, I've faced, losing my first husband unexpectedly was the most difficult one I had ever face in my life. No one expects to lose a loved one at any point in life and it's nothing you can ever be prepared for. However, with God and the support of my family, friends and church family I made it through that loss. Immediately after the loss of my first husband, there was no way I could stay at my house by myself so I moved back home temporarily with my parents. About two weeks after the funeral I discussed with my parents about the need to go back to my house at that time and pack up as many of my clothes and other items in preparation to possibly sell my house at some point. We later went to my house and packed up and stuffed my mom's truck with as much as we could. Once we got back to my parents' house with a truck full of clothes and other storage bends, me and my mom both looked at each other...I shook my head and just did a big sigh. With my mom still looking at me she said, *"YOU WERE BORN FOR THIS!"* I then took a deep sigh and said, "Well mom, yeah! You're right! I was born for this!" I will never ever forget that statement my mom said to me. That was inspiration to me and I was ready to keep it moving!

A Second Chance at Love:

I have been blessed by God with a second chance at love and marriage to my beloved new husband Travis Fowles as of May 30, 2015. Marriage is awesome yet it takes hard work, patience, unconditional love and allowing that room for each other to grow. My mom has been such an awesome example of what a wife truly is. Before I got married again, my mom told me, *"Lisha, when you're married, outside of your relationship with God, your husband is your 1st priority."*

She also told me, *"Don't be so quick to complain to your husband about what you can and can't do. Don't be so quick to make excuses for something you were supposed to do or what you said you would do, but didn't do it."* My mom would also say, *"Don't be so quick to use your period as an excuse for being moody and lashing out or as a crutch for why you can't do something."* This advice has helped me a great deal in my marriage. I learned or should I say I'm still learning from my mom on how to listen and not be so quick to respond or explain and be so defensive when my husband may be addressing an issue with me (Smile).

I've learned from my mom how to open my mouth with wisdom when addressing an issue with my husband. I'm so thankful to God for that because it has helped keep peace in our home.

MAXINE BLACKMON: NESE'S MOM

Nese Hopson

Most stories are probably going to start out with my mom is the best in the world and of course that's how we all feel because most of us have had a wonderful mother. But, I want to say that my mom is an exceptional woman!

She is a very strong and powerful woman, it shows daily, even when she›s a little under the weather.

Psalms 31 verse 10 states: *"...Who can find a virtuous woman? For her price is far above rubies..."*

Throughout her life, she has taught me and my four brothers that God is the refuge and our rock. He wants US to keep our hands in His hands. We have learned from her that if she can get through anything, so can we with God on our side.

Mothers and Women of the Word can be the strength and determination of your success. You are built to stand, you are born in His likeness and no matter what the world throws your way, and you can make it past any situation.

Maxine is her name. She has been through so much and still made it through during the storms of life and taught us that we can do the same. She taught me that you are a lady and must act as one. If God gives you a family use what I have taught you what I have taught you to pass on to them.

My mother has taught me how to have Faith and Hope through anything. She is a wonderful mother and grandmother to not only to our family but to many. There are so many godsons and daughters that she has watched grow into adults. So many students' lives that she has touched over the years. Each will tell you of her gracious love and spirit in their lives. Her lifestyle demonstrates a wealth of Love and knowledge. She is the exemplification of what a true woman of God carries within herself and how it is given to others unselfishly.

She is: Maximum Love, Apple of my Eye, Xtra Ordinary, Independent, Proud Woman and a Nurturing Giver.

BLESSED

Pastor Lowray Bartney

Blessed is the word that comes to mind as I think about this extraordinary woman who is the mother of my male seeds. Using the description of blessed to describe her is found in Proverbs 31:28 (NIV) which reads, "Her children arise and call her blessed; her husband also, and he praises her." This passage of scripture sums up how my sons and I feel about the woman who is our everything. She is our strength when life blows make us feel week. She is our support when life suggests that we give up and walk away from our dreams. She is our shoulder to cry on in our time of weakness; however, she allows us to be weak and she does not belittle, making us feel less than a man. The words that she speaks helps us remember who we are in Christ and how in our weakness He is made strong. Her very words take nothing from us, but only speaks life into us, forcing us to "Man-up".

I often times wonder how she does it. How can one go through life with trials on every side, but continue to stand in joy and peace? She goes through her day without much complaint and she remains consistent in her mind. I am reminded of a conversation we had and she said, "I do not get an opportunity to get weak. When I feel myself wanting to be weak, I immediately think of my family. If I get weak then what will happen to my family?"

I was taken aback by her statement because that showed me the magnitude of how she perceived our family and her intentionality in creating a safe, loving and nurturing environment. When she voiced her concern, I wanted to go internal because I immediately began to think that I was not being the strength to her where she felt that she could not take a moment in time to "be in her feelings."

As we continued to dialogue, she said, "I want you to know that in no way I feel that I am not secure or protected within my family, but I have taken the responsibility to show endurance and strength regardless of what comes our way."

I then began to wonder, If she really had the opportunity to be or show weakness would she actually take it? Would she wallow and complain about all that is plaguing her?

No, I do not believe she would. I believe that God, our creator, built her to stand as a strong tower. She stands poised, strong, tall and with elegance through the tough times. She continues to bubble and smile even through the roughest of times and ultimately her heart's desire is to worship her crowned King through it all.

So, blessed is what we call her. To look at her on the outside, one may never see or realize the weakness that maybe on the inside. I believe that the Lord has blessed her so much that it takes someone that is connected to her and has a spirit of discernment to be able to look into her and pickup what may be deceptive at times. It was not long ago my wife suffered with being a severely anemic where her blood count was terribly low to the point that doctors were wondering how was she able to stand, go to work, walk, sing, take care family, and do everything that she does within her day without passing out. The mere thought of realizing that her body could shut down at any time was mind-blowing because to look at her, she always completed any and all tasks given to her with excellence. She always gave and continues to give 100% in all that she does. I knew without a shadow of a doubt that it was God's GRACE and His BLESSINGS that walked together hand in hand to carry her each and every day. Watching her go through this trying time painted a picture of Isaiah 40:31 which says, "But they that wait upon the Lord shall renew their strength; they shall mount up with wings as eagles; they shall run, and not be weary; and they shall walk, and not faint."

Amazingly, through this entire ordeal, she was able to smile. I found that she would work even harder, not only at home but even with the students she comes into contact on a daily basis at her job. It gives me great pleasure to share this extraordinary woman with her students because I know that she will nurture and care for them just as much as she nurtures and cares for us. She is known not only at home, but in her marketplace.

The early rising and the late setting just to assure that everyone's needs are met is just a part of the fabric of her being. I am extremely grateful. Our boys are extremely grateful that God blessed us with a precious jewel—the one we call Blessed. She continues every day to blow our minds as she walks with GRACE and as the Holy Spirit carries her from Glory to Glory. I, with all confidence know that this woman, mother, wife, daughter, sister and friend will always be blessed.

This is right because BLESSED IS WHAT WE CALL HER. Teddy K, your boy's call you BLESSED.

WISDOM FROM GRANDMA

Agnes Sanders Penny

We were all sitting on the front porch after Sunday services and a sumptuous dinner. I was turning the handle of the ice cream maker, because I was the middle grandchild on the porch. We always took turns making the ice cream machine's handle turn smoothly. My grandmother had her rituals, and Sunday dinners were mandatory if you lived within a one-hundred-mile radius of her home.

"Well, my babies," as Grandma referred to all on the front porch. There were seven grandchildren and seven adults sitting in various swings, chairs, and steps of the old country porch. "It is my time to pass on my pearls of wisdom to you all. You adults can add what you have learned in your life time if you want. Today's topic is how to help choose your future husband or wife, as it might be."

"What do you mean help to choose, Grandma? Don't we get to choose who we want to marry without any interfering from all of you?" Inquired my cousin Bobby, the youngest grandchild on the porch. Bobby was six at the time.

"You never do anything in life without the help of God, Bobby," Grandma replied spitting out some chewing tobacco spit into her small can. "God has His hand in every facet of your life, young man, and he certainly plays a part in helping you choose who you will spend the rest of your life with in this world. Well, that is if you follow my advice of writing down all of the qualities you want in your spouse and putting your list in your personal Bible."

I interjected, "Grandma, that could be a very long list."

"Well, Angel, what would you put on your list?" Grandma asked, looking directly at me.

"Well, I want a man who is tall, handsome, has a good body, has a job, a car, loves to play board games and sports, goes to church, has a dog, has curly hair like mine, loves to go to the movies, loves popcorn, and wants to have a lot of children," I replied, smiling broadly as any seven-year-old would.

Middle Billy added his requirements for a wife, "I want a woman who can cook like you Granny. She has to be shorter than me. She has to know a man is in charge of her life. She has to follow my orders and commands at all times. I want her to be pretty and to have long straight hair like Aunt Flora's. I want her to like children."

"Okay," my mom said. "Here is some notebook paper and some pencils. I want each of you kids to write down what Granny said. Then, I want you to take the note and put it in your personal Bible everyone received during Christmas. Okay, get to writing."

We all wrote for about fifteen minutes. Some of us were on our backs on the porch thinking; while others were writing on hard surfaces like the floor or the seat of a chair. As I remember, we were all in deep thought about this writing assignment.

Grandma continued with her instructions as she looked at each of us lovingly. "You know that you are going to change this list from time to time. But, what I want you to do is to just attach any other lists you make in the future to this first list of qualities you want in a life mate. As you age, your requirements will change with the qualities you desire in a person. Today, I noticed that all of you were listing surface qualities of how a person looked. Your list will grow with more detailed qualities. What I really want you to remember is that by putting this list in your Bible you are asking God for help in finding someone with the qualities you have written down. As you age, God will have an idea of what type of person will fit with you and the qualities you have listed. The person you are seeking may be anywhere in this big round world, and God will make sure that when the time is right, you two will meet. I hope I am alive to see and meet the person God has chosen for each of you. You deserve to have all of your wants and desires come true, and our God will certainly fulfill your wishes."

Every summer, I would stay with my grandmother, my aunt, and my aunt's husband. When my grandmother had some free time, she would ask me to get my Bible to read to her. Oral Bible reading was a tradition in my family as long as I can remember. All of my cousins and I started reading at the age of three, because we had to read a Bible verse every morning to our parents before we washed our faces. We were taught sight reading, and that is how we started reading so early. I brought my Bible out to the kitchen where Grandma was shucking corn.

"Angel, have you updated your husband list for this year?" Grandma asked.

"Yes, Grandma, I have. Do you want to hear some things I have added, because I add things all the time? I have been adding things for years now. This year I will be twelve, and I have been reading a great deal of books, romance and adventure ones. I believe these books have helped me develop my list even more, Grandma," I said proudly.

"Well, let me hear some of the qualities. Some, not all, you hear," She said very quietly.

"Okay. I want my husband to be a gentleman who opens all kinds of doors for me. I want him to be well read, be able to talk about the books he has read, loves me more than his own life;

sees no other woman but me when we are out and about; tells me every day how beautiful I am, takes care of me when I am ill; calls me when he is at work just because; loves and obeys the commandments of God; prays with me every day, loves and cares for his mom, attends church with me every Sunday, and loves the twelve children we will have together." I stopped reading and looked at Grandma.

"Gee, Angel, you are really thinking about your future husband's qualities. You have added great qualities. You are now beginning to look inside the man you will be with for the rest of your life. But, baby, be sure that your husband becomes your friend first. Don't just go for the lust for sex. Please know the man you want to be the father of your children. Get to know his parents. See how he treats his mother, sisters, and female relatives. He must respect the women in his life. Be sure he is patient, loving, and understanding in his nature. Be sure he feels comfortable in his skin. He should be willing to talk to you about anything. Also, become the woman he wants by living a chaste life until he finds you. Just as I am telling you to think about the type of man you want, I pray his granny and parents are doing the same for him. He should be taught to know the type of woman he wants to be his wife and the mother of his children."

"I will remember everything you have said, Grandma," I said cheerfully.

"Please do, baby! A man wants a whole donut, not one that has been bitten into and put back on the shelf. You want your honeymoon night to be very special. You don't want your mind to be comparing your husband to the last guy with whom you had sex. Save yourself for that special man. Don't do more business than the A & P with your body, Angel," Grandma said in a very sullen way.

Even at the age of twelve, I understood what my Grandma was saying about being chaste. I was determined to save my body for my husband.

———

At the end of that summer, I was walking pass the tennis courts at school on my way home, and I saw the most beautiful man in white tennis shorts hitting a tennis ball with his racquet. I could not take my eyes off this young man. I was young, but mesmerized by his movements and his aura. I signed up for tennis as soon as school started, and this beautiful young man became my coach. He was three years older than me, but he became my mentor and friend. He taught me how to deal with school bullies, boys and girls. By the time I was 16, and he was a nineteen-year-old college student, he asked my mom if he could take me out on a date. He was my senior prom date, and we dated off and on for seven years. I kept adding husband qualities every year to my list in my Bible. By the time I was twenty-three, I married my high school sweetheart. We were friends for 42 years, and we were married for 37 years before he died from a massive heart attack. We had two beautiful daughters together, not the twelve children I wanted. But, God's hand was definitely in our getting together. I still have my list in my Bible. Thanks to you, Grandma!

MY MOMMY STORY

Stacie Patterson

I was born to an unwed, 17-year-old teen mom in 1968. I grew up in public housing with my mom, uncle, aunt and grandmother.

My most vivid memory is, at age five, my mom got married and we moved to Kentucky where my stepdad was stationed with the Army. I was miserable. Every time my mom would talk to my grandmother, she would lie and tell me it was a friend so that I wouldn't cry. I stayed in Kentucky a few months before I was returned to my grandmother in NC.

I continued to live with my grandmother while my mom moved on with her life. I saw her on a regular basis; she bought my school clothes, got my hair done, I went on family vacations with her, etc., but I spent most of my time with my grandmother.

I lived with my mom for the first time at 25 years old, after my son's father and I broke up. It was a rocky two years.

I felt that I never added up to her mother standards. Whatever issue I had going on with my son, she had a way of making it feel like it was MY fault. His punishments didn't last long enough, he needed to be in bed on time,... it was always something. I used to think, you didn't raise me so how can you tell me how to raise my child? That's when the resentment started building.

Once we had a blow up and I expressed my feelings. It was during that moment that she first said how she felt as a teen mom with a teen dad who was abusive. She got out of that situation fast!

During my years as a parent, I began to understand more of my mom's fears and frustrations. My feelings of resentment lessened, but weren't gone.

The more we developed relationships with God, the more I began to let go. The more hell my son raised, the closer the bond as we tried to ease his pain. I'm trying to support my child, with my mom trying to support us both. I was still dealing with "mommy issues" because I was trying to teach "tough love" with my son and she kept saying, "My grandson ain't going to be out in the streets." When he would get arrested, she would bond him out.

Until I finally said, "No! I'm trying to save him! Leave his butt in jail." And she listened.

Finally, his antics got me evicted, for a second time. I started looking for a new place. My mother said I could come stay with her, save some money, clean my credit, and buy a home. So, my son and I moved in.

Which bought me to my FB post a few weeks ago as I reflected back...

For the past two mornings, I've dropped my mom off at a conference close to my job. Yesterday morning, she started being nitpicky with, "Why you back out that way?" as I backed out the driveway. I had no comment.

After work, we stopped at the mall. In JC Penney's, I picked up a necklace and earring set. She gave her unsolicited opinion, "I don't like that."

Again, without saying a word, I put it back. Afterward, we drive to Belk's which is on the other side of the mall, because her back hurts and she can't walk that far. I start to park in an empty space and she made her disapproval known because it's not where she usually parks, so I turn around and park in "her" spot.

This morning, we talked about the Domestic Violence Conference she is attending, church, and other small things but she doesn't talk much about my son. I think it hurts too much.

There was a time when I would rebel against everything my mom said to me. I would've bought that necklace, and parked where I wanted. I was also dealing with some past hurts, feelings of abandonment and resentment. Why? Because I wasn't raised by my mom. I didn't grow up in the same house as my siblings and I have unresolved issues with this.

God strategically set it up where I had to come live with my mom so that He could heal "us." God knew it was time for us to completely heal. He even went as far as to subtract my son from the equation and send him on his own personal journey to manhood without "mama" so he would not be a distraction in my healing process.

God and my mommy really loves me! And for that, I'm grateful!

MAMA

Nikki Turner

Generational Strength: Life Lessons

In order for a tree to withstand strong winds, storms and time, it must have a firm foundation; its roots must run deep, deep into the ground; for that's where its strength comes from. I often see myself as a tree, I sway and bend at life's tests and trials, my branches arch as life's storms approach. Although I may lose a branch here, a few leaves there, I have been able to withstand it all... and that's where Mama PJ and the lessons she's taught me come in.

Mama PJ, she is and has always been everything to me; I do mean everything. Not just figuratively, but literally. As do most parents, she wore many hats. I often like to think of those hats, as capes. As a child, I witnessed her do it all, handle life's issues so effortlessly, so swiftly. She never broke a sweat, at least not in front me and my siblings. She would whip one cape off and pop another on and just like that, she would save the day. Swooping down, zooming in on every situation, to fix it, make it right, make it better. I often wondered how she did it all, my mama, my hero, my WONDER woman. In my eyes, she was larger than life. I knew without a doubt that she could do anything, make anything, and fix anything. I don't recall her ever saying, "I can't."

One year for the first day of school, I wanted an original outfit, one that no one else would have. You see, having a new outfit for the first day of school was a big deal and it was original, well that would get me bonus points with my friends. I was heading off to middle school, 6th grade. I really wanted to make a good impression, so I asked mama and just like that, she agreed. We went shopping for fabric; it had to be just right. I remember choosing a polka dot fabric, the background was black and the polka dots were large, bright and multicolored. After we chose the fabric, mama had me help find a pattern. It was on then; my new original outfit was on its way.

Shortly after we arrived home, mama whipped up the cutest pull on shorts, with a matching top. She could work magic with that sewing machine of hers. To this day, I can remember how fancy I felt, how proud I strutted to the bus stop for the first day of school. My friends "oooed" and "aaaahed" over my shorts and top, but the icing on the cake was when I told them my mama made it. That's right, my mama made it! That was one of the many times I realized that my mama, Mama PJ was amazing, I was literally in awe of her. She was my lifeline, my teacher, my provider, my protector, my tutor, my cheerleader, my bodyguard, my seamstress, my hairdresser, my playmate, my dream catcher, my advocate; the list goes on.

Mama was a single parent, but she never let that stop her from achieving whatever the goal was. No complaints were uttered from her mouth, she moved throughout life with an admirable amount of style and grace.

Day in and day out, she created a loving space within the walls we called home, but outside of those walls was very different. We lived in a place where dreams would often go to die, where seeds fell on hardened, dry soil. Never penetrating the earth, never given the opportunity to be nurtured, to grow and meet their full potential. They lay there, drying up, scattered about until they were no more. I watched her stretch herself, watched her scrape the very bottom of the barrel to ensure we had a good home, a happy home, a home filled with love. We were not allowed to utter the words, "I can't". Not only did she tell us we could, she set the example. Mama wasn't afraid to try anything, she wasn't afraid of failure. She would do anything for me and my siblings. Thinking back, I now realize that often times our requests might have been way out there. I can hear us now; "Mama can you make me a dress with matching socks and a headband, by next week? Mama, can we have homemade biscuits with preserves for snack? Mama, can you help me make a wooden lamp for my wood shop class? Mama, I'd love a new handmade cradle for my new baby, can you do that... or Mama can you cook 10 turkeys with sides over the holidays, so that we can feed the homeless?" Many of these requests may have been far-fetched, but Mama got it done! There were times when I'm sure she didn't know how to, but she never said she couldn't and she never said no. If we didn't get a yes, she would say, "I think I can."

———

Seven years ago, I was expecting a baby. I was nesting, you know how that is. Everything needed to be done just right and now, not tomorrow. My husband was trying to put together the baby's crib, as we prepared the final touches on the nursery. We were nearly done when he discovered a problem with one small, but important part of the bed. We contemplated sending it back, but I thought to myself, surely my mama can do this. I called her and explained the issue, I told we didn't have time to send the bed back and wait for a new one. She sighed a bit as I said, "Mama, I know you can fix it. You can fix anything!" I was not attempting to encourage her, as if there was any doubt in my mind. I honestly knew that she could fix it, I KNEW it. She came over, tweaked a piece here, drilled a hole there, and placed a screw there. It was as if I was that 11-year-old girl, watching her mama whip up a new outfit for the first day of school. I was so excited. Again, I was in awe of my mama.

I am not sure if she knew I was watching, always watching as she unknowingly gave me lessons of strength, as she sowed seeds of faith, tenacity, determination a within my spirit. Those seeds would lay there, until I would one day need them. As I grew older, life happened and many a time, I drew from the seeds. When I became a teen mom, unmarried and ashamed; I relied on those seeds. When I decided to pursue my college degree, with twin boys in tow, I drew upon those seeds. When I found myself in an abusive situation, again the seeds mama carefully placed within in me, gave me strength. By the time I was in my early 30's, I'd come to rely and lean on Mama PJ's lessons of strength, quite a bit.

————

Then came September 1st, 2011. On that day, I would withdraw from all mama had taught me, like never before. By this time, I'd gotten married and was pregnant with my fourth child, a baby girl. Just fifteen months ago, I'd given birth to a baby boy. My husband and I were very excited that we had conceived another so soon. The pregnancy was going well, but things took a turn for the worst unexpectedly. My baby girl was born early, very early. She came into this world sixteen weeks prior to her due date, she was barely viable. The outlook was bleak, her chances of survival were very low. For ninety-one days, I sat by my baby girl's incubator, loving on her, praying for her, willing her to live. As I struggled with all of my emotions, fear and doubt tried to overtake me.

One morning, as I was preparing to head to the hospital, a small voice said, "You are Peggy Joyce's daughter, you've got exactly what you need to get through this. That day, I started planting those very seeds within my baby girl. I would open her little incubator and encourage her, tell her how strong she was, how blessed she was. The very seeds that were nestled in my spirit, begin to spill over. The more I spoke them over my baby, the less I struggled with fear and doubt. I started walking into the NICU with confidence, I started encouraging other families who were in the same situation as my family. Thank God for mama and those seeds. I shared them, I planted them, I tossed them to and fro! Seeds of strength, seeds of faith, seeds of hope and healing.

One day mama came to the hospital to sit with me and visit our newest addition. By that time, I'd stop crying about our situation. I was walking by faith; my countenance was up and my smile was back. As we both peered in to look at baby girl, Mama said, "I don't know how you do it. I've watched you handle this situation with so much grace and strength." She was standing behind me with her hand on my shoulder, as I laid my hand on Olivia Rae. I turned with tears in my eyes, looked at Mama and said, "I learned from you. I got my strength from you.

A wise woman once told me that someone is always watching. As we go through our day, our lives, as we deal with life's trials and tribulations, let's always remember that someone is watching. Let's be mindful of the seeds we sow, especially within our children.

BEAUTIFUL BLACK BUTTERFLY: GOD'S ORIGINAL DREAMKEEPER

Monique Thomas

Two groups of siblings were born to a woman in sets of five. The first five were born to the woman when she was young in age and young in her understanding of knowledge. Her husband was a military man who had served his country proudly and used his wages to pay himself first into savings and then he sent a portion home to his wife to run their household. When he returned to his family, he did so with a pension and the accumulated savings, which he used to purchase farming land and start two businesses. The entire first set of five children worked the farm alongside their parents. The husband and wife ran a catering business and the father and sons ran a trash removal business.

Sarah Grace was the youngest of the ten children. She was born last of the second set of five. Her sisters called her the "baby butterfly". The story of her birth was told often. Sarah Grace's earliest memory was of hearing the story of her birth told while she sat on her oldest brother's work boot. She wrapped herself into a cuddle around the shin of his right leg, and once she was secure, he would slowly rock his leg to and fro as he began to tell the following story:

One day, three of the younger brothers found a periwinkle

caterpillar, while they rested under the protection of the shade of the mighty oaks. The boys shouted across the farm to their sisters to bring a mason jar from the top of the ice cooler. While they waited, one broke a branch from a tree and held a small broken segment of the broken branch close to the caterpillar. However, the piece of wood was still too large, so the middle brother picked up a twig from the ground, and held it near the caterpillar so that it could slowly inch its way onto the twig. Once the jar arrived, the boys slowly and easily placed the tiny creature into the jar, which would become its new habitat filled with some leaves and a sponge soaked with sugar water. The sisters had already used an ice pick to poke holes into the lid. Then the brothers screwed the lid on top of the jar to keep the caterpillar safely inside of its new home. They could all hear their mama's words traveling as whispers along the breezes across the fields saying, "Oh my! It sounds like those children are at the larval stage of retelling the story of the Birth of the Beautiful Black Butterfly."

The youngest brother hollered, "Yes Mama, the caterpillar is already in its new home, and it is about to begin spinning dizzily to make a cocoon as it hangs upside down from the tip of the angel's finger." Then he stands up to joyously demonstrate his ability to become dizzy as he threw up his arms and began to spin around and around.

The older sisters were already in route to take their seats beside their brothers and Sarah Grace. Just as they arrive the youngest brother stopped spinning and sat in his sister's lap with his head bent over his knees in the shape of a teardrop. The older brother continued to tell the story and mentioned. "It seems as if our young brother is feeling all shook up and woozy much like the pupa that is now in the jar instead of the caterpillar. At this stage the pupa, must go through the physical stress and pain of body changes that occur during metamorphosis."

Just then the older brother began to shake Sarah Grace almost awry from his boot. Yet she hung on and giggled as he continued to describe how she wriggled inside their mama, like the pupa with newly formed tiny wings inside of a chrysalis trying to break free. It was not long before the new young Black Beautiful Butterfly appeared into this new world as everyone who came to see her stared in amazement at God's glorious transformed creature. She wearily started out by merely lifting her wings. In time, and with continued practice, the "Beautiful Black Butterfly" grew regular habits and followed familiar motions until she was able to spread her wings. When that day came, all the family gathered to open the jar so that the "Beautiful Black Butterfly", known as Sarah Grace, could be released from her small habitat and go freely into the world filled with the promise of being a Dream keeper.

She shall go forward sharing the knowledge, wisdom, and understanding that she and every future generation that descends from her, that they are an original gift from God.

May all the women who gather together be familiar with Romans 12:2 "Don't copy behavior and customs of this world, but let God transform you into a new person by changing the way you think. Then you will learn to know God's will for you, which is good and pleasing and perfect."

FIRST MY MOTHER—FOREVER MY FRIEND

Parris Solomon

A mother to many of us, can be seen as a precious gift from God. Many of us like to think moms are created to love, to nurture, to build, to provide, and the list goes on and on. These are just a few of the duties that being a mom is called to do. All of these things mentioned were found in my mother. I thank God for blessing me with a mom that showed me that I was created for a purpose and then showing me how to become that purpose.

Early on in my life, my mom always laid a Christian foundation to her children. I believe my siblings, Johnny and Coleta would agree with me. My mother always made sure that we knew who God was and I can never forget that. This has always kept me in a safe place with Him. I always knew that He would be there for me and He has until this day, kept His word. She is the one who is deserving of this impartation into my life. As a mother, you are to make sure that you bring your child up in the word of God and she has honestly did that. Not only has she done so by instilling this in her children but she has demonstrated through her life.

Without a shadow of a doubt, I can truly say that my mother is a faithful servant of the Lord our God. She seeks Him in everything she does. She puts Him first. She impacts many around her through song, prayer, and ministering the word. Some years ago, my mother accepted her call into the ministry and became an evangelist, further speedily leading to her ordination as an Elder of the church. The fire that she has inside of her radiates so much that you know that she serves a God who is of honor and recognition.

My mother also exhibits many other outstanding characteristics. Skillfully, she is also a hard worker. Her hands are blessed and everything she touches practically turns into gold. She works while it is day as she knows that when night comes, no man can work. Having providing for her family, she always made sure that her children, all of whom are adults now, have what they need. She seeks to do those same things for her grandchildren as well. I believe that she knows that her duty is to help provide for her family and she does so without complaining. She gives freely to those in need. She is an excellent cook and feed many people in her community no matter what day it is. She does so with service and gratitude. She enjoys serving in her church and wears many hats.

Wherever she is needed in the ministry, she will serve tirelessly. She never hesitates and is always ready when you call on her. It is my pleasure to write this in honor of her. I believe that one should be told how much they touch and impact others in their life. It is called giving honor where honor is due. She should know that her work goes unnoticed. If I could give her all the very desires of her heart, I would do so without hesitation. What I will promise her is that I will always follow the voice and heart of God. In that, you cannot put a price on.

Most know that my mom is very outspoken but seems to be often misunderstood. She believes in speaking the truth and she will do so, with no intentions of finding fault. She doesn't believe that one should be held in their wrong, as this is not the will of the Father. She can come across strong but mean no harm by it.

There are some that have taken her kindness for granted, yet she still does not hold it against them and still aim to love with the love of Christ inside her.

My mother has to be the strongest person I know. I have seen her go through some things, most couldn't have. She never showed her children any weak side of her. When I look at her, I see strength. I see a woman that has been through many storms but shows no evidence of it ever taken place. She knows where her help comes from. She depends on God to see her though the rough patches and knows he carries her every step of the way.

Though she has endured some turbulent times, we have also celebrated many of her accomplishments down thru the years. Recently, my mom earned her Bachelor's Degree in Early Childhood Education from the University of Mount Olive. I was so happy to have witnessed her reaching and accomplishing one of her aspirations. In awe, I recall thinking, The Lord did it again! He allowed her to accomplish one of her heart's desires. Alongside this, she is the proud owner of The Children of Joy Childcare Center in Eastern, NC, another ministry God has entrusted her to.

One of her many passions are working with kids. She also finds joy in working with the elderly population as this is her most cherished highlights of her career. I watched her serve in that capacity for over 30 years. God has allowed her to travel back to the same nursing center she worked at for years to minister to his people.

Look at God!

Her work truly speaks for itself. Wherever He leads her, she follows without missing a beat. His spirit rests upon her and if you are ever around her, you can truly fill the power of God on her. I strive to be the God-fearing lady that she is and pray that I can impact many just as she has and does. She deserves all that her heart can hold. Her dedication to God's people in the ministry is endearing.

Again, I thank God for her life and pray that she has plenty more countless years to serve, to impact, to lead, and to continue in her purpose that He most righteously has for her. Mom, I love you with all my heart and hope that you find that this is only a smidgen of all the things that I can say about you. You are my Rock, a friend like no other, and a prayer warrior of the most high!

Continue down the path of righteousness, your victory awaits! I know surely on that great day, you will be handed your crown of glory! Oh what a day that will be! Continue to live your life fully for the sweet name of Jesus! Your work is not in vain! May your blessings continue to overtake you!

AFTERWORD

It is a special calling to be a mother. It the highest level, God-given responsibility given a woman who is still in self-discovery. This role, motherhood, may appear comfortable or easy to those on the outside looking in because the physical demands in comparison do not appear to be as great. However, just ask the mother of eight how difficult it is to lift those babies, day in and day out, how demanding it can be on her physically and mentally. This can often be a thankless job whilst the mom is in the throes of mothering and doing much of the hard work. Honestly, it is not until a child has become the parent do they REALLY begin to appreciate all the sacrifices that a mother has makes.

Some may not think that being a mother requires intelligence. However, a wise and discerning mom knows precisely what to say when it is needed. She also knows enough to point her children to God's heart, leave them there, and let Him lead them the rest of the way. Now, to do this definitely requires a high level of intelligence. You have to be smart enough to persuade the minds of hungry children that what is prepared, no matter how little it is, that what is prepared is a feast; especially when she knows it's really only enough for one. She is intelligent enough to help her children dream the impossible even when she does not have a clue how they will accomplish it. She naturally wants them to have, be, and do better. She is intelligent in ways that are simply immeasurable.

Being a mother doesn't come with a manual. We do the best with the tools we have been given. It is my hope that as we are able to get better information, we are then able and willing to accept, and then correct some of the mistakes of our own childhood. We should not want erroneous philosophies and understandings to continue to be taught and consequently repeated in the next generation. Something transformational occurs when a woman discovers that she is with child. No matter what the mother is enduring, her mind instinctively analyzes her life to see how she is able to welcome a newborn. For some, the sense of family and community make this a joyous time. For others, pregnancy is scary and often daunting.

I think that from the happiest and most delightful of these stories to the dark and deeply disturbing ones, there is a common underlying theme; good Mothers are dedicated to help their children thrive regardless of how inferior their upbringing. Some are able to do this better than others are. Nevertheless, we all pattern our behavior based upon what we have seen or experienced. When we learn better, it is our hope that we will do better.

It is impossible to teach what you do not understand. What I do know for sure though is that somewhere in a child's pure and hopeful heart, no matter how inadequate a mother may be is a deep and unexplainable love for her.

To Moms, do not live your life in regret. You deserve all the love, generosity, thankfulness and more. Sure, every mother can look back and wish we had made different choices. But for some of us, we were in REAL survival mode. So, as we would say to those we meet in counseling for the first time,

I'm so glad you made it!

I'm so glad your children made it!

By the Grace of God, you made it!

You survived and so did your Seed!

Did you hear me?!

Your seed made it!

Now Trust the vinedresser (Jesus) to develop it into what He desires.

Enjoy the fruit of your labor and delivery... LOL!

I pray a special blessing upon everyone who reads this book.

May you have the courage to forgive yourself as God has forgiven you.

I decree and declare, that the every estranged relationship between the children and parents be restored NOW in Jesus' name. You will walk in divine forgiveness and compassion.

Open the eyes of the readers so that they understand that being a Mother doesn't come with a manual. Some mistakes and wrong decisions will be made. We do the best with what information we have. Your love and grace covers the rest.

Decide today to write out what you desire to see in your life. Create a written plan today for your life.

Your generations will be blessed by the new information and new decisions you make now.

Trust God.

Do your cest.

Love your children.

Love and cherish your mother and Mother's your children.

Learn to cook and clean (It helps).

Take care of your husband (smile).

Don't fuss about cleaning the house so much that you don't have time to spend making great memories.

At the end of the day....

Don't worry.

Run a hot tub of water, get it in a while, and then.... Lay across the bed.

God is going to have to take care of most of the stuff we worry about anyway.

Love ya,
Phenomenal Women and Mothers

Made in the USA
Columbia, SC
16 April 2019